# THE *Bluffer's*® GUIDE TO
# GOLF

D1343135

Adam Ruck

*Bluffer's*®

Colette House
52-55 Piccadilly
London W1J 0DX
United Kingdom

Email: info@bluffers.com
Website: bluffers.com
Twitter: @BluffersGuide

First published 1987
This edition published 2013
Copyright © Bluffer's® 2013

Publisher: Thomas Drewry
Publishing Director: Brooke McDonald

Series Editor: David Allsop
Design and Illustration by Jim Shannon
With kind acknowledgments to Peter Gammond,
author of earlier editions of *The Bluffer's Guide to Golf*

A CIP Catalogue record for this book
is available from the British Library.

ISBN: 978-1-909365-32-2 (print)
      978-1-909365-33-9 (ePub)
      978-1-909365-34-6 (Kindle)

# CONTENTS

Golfers can be quite difficult, withdrawn and hard to talk to, especially in the build-up, during and after an important game – in other words, all the time.

# THE NEVER-ENDING PAGEANT

You may think you understand what PG Wodehouse described as 'that never-ending pageant, which men call Golf,' well enough to hold your own when conversation around the dinner table settles on the game's inexhaustible fascination. Don't get over-confident – nobody fully understands golf.

Mark Twain is credited with describing it as 'a good walk spoiled', but he might have missed the point. It's not just about spending long hours tramping around an elaborate obstacle course competing to hit a small ball into a series of small holes.

Golf is the bluffer's game *par excellence* at all levels of ability and experience. At its simplest, it is about pretending to be a better golfer than you are. At its most advanced and calculating, it is about bluffing your way to victory, or at least a less ignominious defeat, in any number of ways that come under the broad umbrella of psychological warfare. Your greatest strength is the extent to which you are successful in reading and playing your opponent (not the ball).

By your words, actions, body language, deployment

of the rule book and even your choice of outfit, you can bluff your adversary into using the wrong club, conceding a putt or accepting a penalty. You can inspire in him* thoughts of self-fulfilling defeatism or lift him up to an exalted plane of fatal over-confidence. You may even be able to bluff yourself into playing a better shot. All of these invaluable tricks of the trade will be explained in the pages that follow, along with the basic technical and background information about golf and its culture required for the armchair golfer to pass muster in polite society.

---

Becoming proficient at golf requires
an investment of more time and money
than most of us can justify.

---

Will golf make you a better person? Nothing could be less certain. It may well have the opposite effect, rendering you disappointed, bitter and considerably poorer than you might otherwise have been when you count the cost of

---

* Gender matters. Golf is a game of few words, or should be. It is in this spirit of economy, and not out of any gender bias, that we have employed the shorter and simpler forms 'he', 'him' and 'man' in preference to the longer 'he and/or she', 'him and/or her' and 'man and/or woman'. As any bluffer will tell you, egalitarianism is alive and well on the golf course. Though not necessarily in the clubhouse…

membership subscriptions, green fees, Kevlar-reinforced rescue clubs, self-propelling electric trolleys, miracle-fibre breathable waterproofs, lost bets, hefty supplements for air travel, divorces and missed opportunities to earn an honest living. Golfers can be quite difficult, withdrawn and hard to talk to, especially in the build-up, during and after an important game – in other words, all the time.

They say golf reveals character like no other sport; 'they' being people who are good at golf and inclined to win. Those who are less good at the game find this so-called truth less convincing, or at least less comfortable. Golf doesn't reveal character so much as the injustice of life, the world, everything really.

But there is an undeniable correspondence between a player's behaviour during the course of a golf match and his real self. Are you a bag half-full sort of golfer, or bag half-empty? If the jury had played golf with OJ Simpson (*see* 'Passing Muster at the Club', page 72), would it have seen the real person and would its verdict have therefore been different? Does the sight of your ball in an awkward position that could easily be improved by a discreet nudge of the toecap make you wonder if anyone is watching and think: 'why not?'

In the end, it matters little if golf does or does not reveal character accurately. It is widely believed to do so, and it follows that the better you are perceived to be at golf, the more favourably people will look on you.

Unfortunately, becoming proficient at golf requires an investment of more time and money than most of us can justify, as well as an early start in life, as enjoyed by Tiger Woods, Rory McIlroy and other child prodigies whose mothers fed them baby food with a cut-down spoon or wedge. (As you are about to find out, these are both names for lofted clubs deemed to be among the easiest to use). If you are reading this book, as opposed to having it read to you as a child, it is almost certainly too late to take up the game with any hope of satisfaction.

So, like the rest of us, you will have to bluff. And here you enter perilous territory, which is where this short guide can offer invaluable help. It sets out to conduct you through the main danger zones encountered in discussions about golf, and to equip you with a vocabulary and evasive technique that will minimise the risk of being rumbled as a bluffer. It will give you a few easy-to-learn hints and methods that might even allow you to be accepted as a golfer of rare ability and experience. But it will do more. It will give you the tools to impress legions of marvelling listeners with your knowledge and insight – without anyone discovering that, until you read it, you probably didn't know the difference between a Scargill and a Brazilian.

# 1744 AND ALL THAT

Golf's origins are shrouded in the mists and mishits of time and need not detain the bluffer long. It is polite to affect a respectful awareness of the history of the game, but too close a preoccupation may mark you out as a nerd.

Nonetheless, you should have a certain basic familiarity with its origins. Golf began in Scotland, and remains a Scottish verb – 'to golf'. It is an essentially Scottish game which should be played in a stiff breeze over nice firm turf – on the cusp between pasture and tundra – at a pace sufficient to keep the blood flowing but without excessive wind chill. One of the game's great drawbacks is the amount of space required per player – many thousands of square feet – compared with bridge (3 sq ft) or squash (just under 700 sq ft). You might mention the latter if only to provide an opportunity to quote the modern American satirist PJ O'Rourke who, in pointing out that golf is a superior game to squash, observed that: 'You can smoke or drink on a golf course without interrupting the game, and you can take a leak – something you can't do on a squash court and shouldn't do in a swimming pool.'

Golf thus requires a sparsely populated region and preferably one with a harsh climate. Scotland – or at least its coastline, the only part of the country with the right type of grass – is ideal. Not many people fancy golf or any other outdoor activity on a typical Scottish summer's day, to say nothing of spring, and this keeps the courses nice and empty, allowing the game to flow.

Irish golfing conditions are similar – not quite so cold, but wetter – and the game took an early hold there too, on the coast once again, the interior being waterlogged. On the testing Lancashire coast, or Fylde, it is often said that if you can't see the Pennines it's raining; and if you can, you should have your eye on the ball. This is another golfing heartland.

Over time, golf mania led to the demand for courses in drier and warmer locations such as Berkshire, the south of Spain and the south of France, where renegades from Wellington's Scottish brigades not unreasonably put down roots on their way home from the Battle of Salamanca in 1812. Who can blame them?

Whether it was golf, marriage, diplomacy, or some other confrontation that the dashing nineteenth-century Prussian soldier and philosopher Carl von Clausewitz described as 'war by other means', the game has its origins in the perennial conflict between England, Scotland, France and other fringe participants in what is now known as the Six Nations Championship (it's a rugby contest apparently).

**1421** At the Battle of Baugé, during the drinks interval, the French entertain (or thrash) their Scottish allies (or mercenaries) at 'chole,' a hockey-like contest played with sticks and balls. The Scots take chole back to Scotland and rename it 'hole.' A new sport is born. One day it will be renamed GOLF, a multi-purpose acronym if you prefer Gentlemen Only, Ladies Forbidden; Game of Limitless Frustration; Great Opportunity to Lose Friends, etc. The actual etymological provenance of the name is uncertain.

**1457** Golf is banned by King James II because it is too much fun to be allowed in Scotland. Also, it distracts the soldiery from archery. This misguided ban (could there be a better preparation for the longbowman than flighting a 3-iron into the Scottish wind?) was repeated in the early 1470s and again in 1491, so it was obviously disregarded.

**1561** Marie Stuart, a keen golfer, crosses the Channel to become Mary, Queen of Scots, bringing with her several young male escorts or 'cadets', who compete to lift up her skirts and carry her clubs during the game, dispensing gallantries such as 'nice ankle turn, ma'am', 'ne'er up, ne'er in' and 'perchance milady may receive a stroke at this hole'. Soon, all fashionable golfers want their own cadet.

**1567** Mary is in trouble for playing golf too soon after the murder of her most recent husband. This is hardly fair. Several hours had elapsed.

**1590** Sir Walter Raleigh drops his coat in casual water (a temporary hazard on the course) and invents smoking. Golf becomes even more fun, and Elizabeth I probably became the first golf widow.

**1593** John Henrie and Pat Rogie are imprisoned for 'playing of the gowff on the links of Leith every Sabbath the time of the sermonses.' Who were they? (Keen golfers, probably. This is a relatively oft-cited early golf trivia fact. PG Wodehouse dedicated his golf book, *Golf Without Tears: Stories of Golfers and Lovers*, to them). Sunday

---

♛

18 holes is enough for a good start to go disastrously wrong and for a hopeless duffer to fluke a par.

---

gowffers seek to avoid detection by carrying the club upside down between shots and pretending it's a walking stick. Hence the term: 'Sabbath sticks'.

**1603** After a game at Musselburgh, James VI travels south to become James I and doubtless draws up plans for the first Anglo-Scottish Golfing Union. Golf would soon be played on Blackheath in south-east London, and one day as far as Sandwich.

**1618** James VI/I grants his subjects the right to play golf on Sundays.

**1620** 100 puritans, unwilling to remain in a country so licentious and debauched as to permit Sunday golf, set sail for America. Golf spreads like wildfire over there, but not for another eight-or-so generations.

**1744** The Gentleman Golfers of Edinburgh organise the first championship and write the first set of *Rules of Golf.* The 13 commandments include 'your tee must be upon the ground' – a rule worth bearing in mind to this day.

**1754** The Society of St Andrews Golfers is founded and decides to call its home town the 'Home of Golf'. 80 years later it renames itself the Royal and Ancient Golf Club (R&A) and takes over the government of golf everywhere except the USA, where different rules apply. This schism may explain why the Ryder Cup (*see* page 95) is such an argumentative event.

**1764** St Andrews converts its golf course from 22 holes to 18. David Hume, Adam Smith and other enlightened Scottish thinkers understand that a game of golf can only go for so long: 18 holes is enough for a good start to go disastrously wrong and for a hopeless duffer to fluke a par, and is as much golf as a man wants to play between an optimistic kippers-and-oatmeal breakfast and drowning his sorrows in whisky at lunchtime. 18 holes therefore became the allotted span, and courses have been designed this way ever since. Sometimes they go out and back, at other times back and out, or even round and round. No one cares, as long as they end at the clubhouse.

**1800s** Golf spreads to all corners of the British Empire. The conquest of Malaya led to the invention of the gutta-percha (gutty) ball which replaced the elegant but expensive and ineffectual 'featherie', which was a leather pouch stuffed with goose or chicken feathers. You will do your bluffing credentials no harm by knowing that gutta-percha is the latex produced from a tree commonly found in Malaysia. For many years all gutty balls were handmade.

In the early days, the golf ball was smooth. Later, golfers noticed that as balls became old and battle-scarred, they flew faster and farther. (In 1905 William Taylor added a pock-marked or dimple pattern to the ball at the manufacturing stage.)

Tee technology proceeded apace. Until the late nineteenth century, golfers filled their pockets with sand and, when permitted to tee the ball, placed it on top of a carefully constructed mound. This took ages, and besides, golfers felt that the quarries (or bunkers) they excavated for teeing sand were large enough and further digging would only make the game more difficult, which ran contrary to the constructive spirit of the tee. Another solution was urgently required.

**1889** First portable golf tee is patented by Scottish golfers William Bloxsom and Arthur Douglas. The not very snappily named Bloxsom Douglas would soon face stiff competition from the Perfectum (rubber tee with a metal spike) and the ultimately victorious Victor (not very different from the Perfectum, but with a cup-shaped top). Bluffers who attempt to impress playing companions, friends and family by reviving the Perfectum v Victor debate may not always find a receptive audience.

**1891** The R&A achieves the long-overdue standardisation of the golf hole on the green. It would be the size of the first ever 'hole cutter' developed by the greenkeepers of Musselburgh, a municipal links course near Edinburgh, in 1829. Legend tells us that this revolutionary invention was fashioned from a section of drainage pipe left lying around the green. The diameter was 4.25 inches, which just happens to be the diameter of the golf hole used around the world today. One way or another, the final agreed size was almost certainly arrived at arbitrarily.

**1914-1945** Two world wars had little impact on Europe's best golf courses.

**1961** Carter Bros Rug Co of Chattanooga, Tennessee, invents the Cocktail Golf rug 'for golfing executives who practise putting in the office.' This brightens up office life to no end and solves absenteeism at a stroke. 'The miniature three-hole golf course is a textured rug made of nylon with a putting course laid out in different colors and pile depths. The holes are three soft rubber practice cups. There's a built-up rough around the edge, a smooth, flat fairway, depressed sand traps and even a water hazard in the center.' The Cocktail Golf rug is a precious bluffing collectable, more highly prized than even the cocktail flagstick.

**1962** With the continuing technological advancement of the golf buggy, golf's evolution was almost complete. The Ramble-Seat model ('for shopping, golf – and fun!'), for instance, was made for the average-sized American golfer, but needed an extra power pack and trailer before his golf bag, soda fountain and hot dogs could be accommodated.

Bluffers must deplore the golf buggy, and you should complain about being forced to use them on courses (mostly foreign) with steep hills between holes.

**1971** Research and development begins on the golf ball that won't slice; it uses an asymmetric dimple pattern to ensure a self-correcting flight path. Marketed as the Polara a few years later, it was soon banned (like most things that make golf easier).

**1980s-on** Anything that makes golf easier is similarly banned. In perpetuity.

# GET THE LOOK

There was a time when the golfer, setting out for a day's sport, could pack with a degree of confidence. For the game, a set of golf clothes. For the clubhouse, a jacket; a shirt with buttons, collar, and links-themed cuffs; a school, club, regimental or other tie of subdued colour, non-humorous design and free of propaganda related to sexual orientation, politics or Christmas; a pair of tidy trousers with belt, braces or the full set; and dark socks and leather shoes. Today, shockingly, there are golf clubs where you would be less conspicuous in flip-flops, pyjama bottoms, a Mohican hairstyle and a Black Sabbath T-shirt. And not having shaved for a week.

Faced with such uncertainty, the traditional principles of functional golf clothing are worth remembering.

## OUTER GARMENTS

The trousers should be loose-fitting to allow complete freedom of movement, with hip swivel and knee snap; and must not get bogged down in the mud when playing out of a knee-deep water hazard. The obvious answer is the 'plus fours', a pair of trousers that end four inches below the knee (hence the name) and known in the USA, inexplicably, as 'knickers'. The sock should meet the trouser and secure it, to exclude any risk of an ugly gap.

Above the waist, similar considerations apply, with the need for pockets. The Norfolk jacket has never been bettered. The more traditional long red frock coat is still common in Wimbledon, but exposes you to the threat of attack from the anti-hunt lobby.

♛

As long as you are not
dressed in anything too bright,
no one will notice you.

To wear any such uniform today, however, risks branding you a fancy-dress golfer, or a member of a curious antiquarian golf society. That might be a good bluff, but there are quite a few real ones about and you might easily be handed a 'cleek' (*see* Glossary, page 115) and invited to show off your skills, leading to almost certain exposure.

The best that can be said is that these days almost anything goes. Shorts are widely worn in the summer months, and it is no use pretending otherwise. The tie is rarely seen, bared knees proliferate, and the long-sock rule, where it is still enforced in plush suburban locations such as the RAC, has ceased to be a serious attempt to maintain standards and become little more than an excuse for a reprimand.

Embrace freedom! Forget that golfing cliché, the diamond-patterned Pringle sweater. As long as you are not dressed in anything too bright, no one will notice you. Bear in mind that your clothing on and off the course, your golf bag, its contents and all other costume props must strike one considered style note. Shun if possible all logoed clothing or brands that employ the vulgar external label (unless you have a good sponsorship deal on the go), and make understatement your keynote. But stuff a tie in your pocket, just in case.

## SHOES

The same goes for golf shoes. Nothing is as it was. Even spikes have gone soft. The two-tone perforated Gatsby, with matching bag and glove, will identify you as a cheat, a fraud and a hustler of dubious provenance, but (spikes permitting) there is still a place for the external flapping leather tongue that conceals the laces (or absence thereof). Prioritise comfort, while bearing in mind that a winter shoe with a summer trouser is not a good look. Spiked rubber ankle boots are available on the Continent, and are worth taking to Ireland.

## GLOVES

Glove, in fact. The golfer wears only one – in the rear trouser pocket – with one finger protruding defiantly, or two in a V configuration. Left or right pocket, depending on the coded socio-sexual message you are intending to send out.

## HATS

Let variety be your watchword. The golf bag is there to be filled, and have hats attached to it. A brightly coloured baseball cap has sponsorship potential and annoyance value, and a long peak to disguise your intentions when you want to sneak a look at your opponent's club selection. The Australian bush hat menacingly worn by Greg Norman has attachments for corks popped during the round. If you favour the bobble hat, go the whole bobble. Make sure the bobble is very bobbly, loosely attached and large so that you can bobble it just as your opponent is about to play. There is no need for a bell, which may cross the line between tactics and crime. The bowler, admittedly a curious look on the golf course, is useful for all sorts of odd jobs, including the decapitation of camera-clicking spectators and ugly statues overlooking the green. The golfer can never have too many hats. The hatless brim and capless peak come into the category of ladies' wear.

## LADIES' WEAR

This is best left to ladies. They have always enjoyed greater latitude than their male counterparts at golf clubs, and that is as it should be, on Tuesday afternoons.

Having said that, few male golfers are averse to the juxtaposition of white ankle socks and a well-cut golf skirt. (On a woman, preferably).

## WATERPROOFS

A light set for showers, a medium set for average rainfall, and a heavy-duty set of trawlerman's oilskins for Ireland.

Don't expect even these to keep the rain out. Several towels are essential: one for the clubs, another for the hands and face, a third to dry the towels. Some bluffers will not bother with waterproofs, shedding layers as the sky darkens, and declaring blithely, 'In wet weather, less is more.' This strategy may lead to pneumonia.

## UMBRELLA

The golfing umbrella is huge, as is necessary to conceal any adjustments you need to make to the position of your ball in the rough. It is made of panels of contrasting primary colours. A plain-coloured or downright colourless umbrella would

---

The golfing umbrella is huge, as is necessary to conceal any adjustments you need to make to the position of your ball in the rough.

---

be much less effective as a decoy or visual distraction, when put up at vital moments and sent bowling down the fairway in a high wind. It also helps to offer sponsors a selection of different colours when selling advertising in an attempt to offset golf costs. Against a backdrop of 'Buy a Volvo', bunker play is almost impossible. The umbrella does not count against your allowance (14 clubs), unless you play a shot with it.

## SUNGLASSES AND SPF STUFF

For extreme weather, a good skin cream and eye protection should be carried. Sunglasses add an element of inscrutability that the bluffer may find tempting. But you may want to think twice as the example of David Duval illustrates. After winning the 2001 Open Championship to cement his position among the world's very top pro golfers, Duval tied up a deal with Oakley and transformed his on-course persona from that of everyday sporting superstar to cold mafia hitman. In two years his ranking slumped to 211th in the world and, still contractually bound to wearing his branded sunglasses at all times, he took a break from golf. Maybe a more understated pair of Primark Sport Pro (RRP £1.99) would have got the job done more effectively. Or it could be that sunglasses just don't help.

## EXTREME SURVIVAL GEAR

A round of golf is a long walk in the wilderness, and the risk of losing, and getting lost, is ever present. Be prepared, with a bottle of something sustaining and some basic rations. A lightweight tent, a thermal blanket, a signalling device like a Verey pistol, a small foghorn and a few fireworks are optional extras.

## ORIENTEERING

The well-prepared golfer will also carry some light reading, detailed charts of the course with contours, trig points and water hazard depths; spare scorecards plus a little pad with a clip to put them in; a gross of all-weather pencils (HB), evenly distributed around the pockets; and an up-to-date dictionary of Gaelic-English street invective to translate the caddie's instructions. The golf bag (*see* 'Tools of the Trade', page 25) will expand to accommodate a full and rich lifetime of pitchmark repair tools, five-year golfing diaries, Bluffer's Guides and other much-valued Christmas presents.

In years to come, you may find that you have been carrying around in some remote recess of your golf bag half a bottle of whisky, several pairs of decaying gloves, a family of field mice and three sets of car keys.

# TOOLS OF THE TRADE

Before you even think of setting foot on the first tee (for absolute beginners, that's the raised section of the golf course in full view of smirking members in the clubhouse bar), you must have a rough idea of the appropriate golfing equipment with which to arm yourself.

The positive bluffing approach is to splash out on the best of everything, the idea being to put a less well-equipped golfer at a psychological disadvantage. This is expensive, requires extra outlay on a caddie, trolley or electric buggy, won't make you play any better, and leaves you with no excuse for bad play. However, it is important for the bluffer to adopt the approach that suits his personality. If you are the sort of person, like Mr Toad, whose interest in a new hobby is directly related to the shopping opportunities it affords, do not hold back.

## BAGS

In the early days of the sport, before golfers took the hint from Roman frescoes showing the goddess Diana with a bag of arrows slung over her shoulder, clubs were carried in a bundle under one arm, by a slave or caddie (from the French 'cadet'; *see* previous chapter). These days, caddies are confined to courses whose target market is brokerage golfers, bogus heritage seekers, film stars and Premiership footballers. Even if you like the idea of paying a spotty teenager £50 to insult you, you should not rely on being able to find one everywhere you go. Although the reintroduction of compulsory caddies as a youth employment scheme is under consideration in Whitehall, for the moment you will need a golf bag of some kind.

The most likely choice will be an enormous faux-leather receptacle with zip pockets all over it, the largest designed to hold the innumerable volumes of the *Rules of Golf*. A free-standing bag of this kind works well for bluffing in the home, as an umbrella/tennis racket/fishing rod stand prominently sited in the hall. It will also hold any small trees you might want to grow in the conservatory. In years to come, you may find that you have been carrying around in some remote recess of your golf bag half a bottle of whisky, several pairs of decaying gloves, a family of field mice and three sets of car keys.

Gone are the days when golfers bought equipment from the pro shop at the golf club. Only fools, millionaires and those who have left home without their shoes and waterproofs do this, but if the persona you wish to adopt is that of the carefree plutocrat, buying a new set of top-of-the-range Callaways with matching accessories will have the desired effect. Regular golfers go to golf supermarkets in places like Croydon and Myrtle Beach, or do their shopping online.

However, if you join a club, even as a weekday non-playing country member, it is a good idea to have the club professional (universally known as the 'pro') on your side, and to this end you may decide to buy a small bottle of water and a Twix, albeit overpriced, before setting out. This will stand you in good stead and establish you on 'Good morning, George' terms, to impress and put off any guests you may invite in the future.

As well as asking the pro's advice about golf clubs (which you will buy cheaply online later), keen golfers poke around the second-hand section of the pro shop, especially at smart clubs like Sunningdale where members (Sean Connery, Gary Lineker, Tim Henman) trade in their drivers, irons and putters for new ones every other week. 'Bought them at (enter club name here)', you can then say of a new set. 'Apparently (enter celeb name here) found they were rather too technically demanding for his game and traded them in for something a little more forgiving.'

## CLUBS

Do not make the mistake of using too many clubs. Four will do, but most golfers interpret the 14-club allowance to mean a full set of 14 is essential to play well. This is very far from the truth. All you need is a wood for long shots, a wedge for short shots and bad spots, an iron for in-between shots, and a putter. Anyone armed with such an assortment would probably score well and gain quite a reputation. Tied together with an elastic band, the short set is easily carried, but it takes a good bluffer to carry it off.

The numbers on clubs are supposed to be a guide to help you decide which to carry. As a rule of thumb (certainly not endorsed by manufacturers and pro shops), multiply the club by three, and if higher than your handicap (*see* 'Handicaps (and Gamesmanship)', page 45), you can use it. Thus, according to this rule, an 18-handicap golfer should not use anything lower than a 6-iron, and only single-figure handicappers should attempt the 3. Try not to get confused between the 6 and the 9.

♛

> The novice golfer's usual mistake is to carry too many balls. This is self-fulfilling defeatism, and no bluffer should encumber himself with more than six.

There are different rules for woods and wedges. For example, many female golfers have such high handicaps that they carry no irons at all, using strange weapons such as the 9-wood for their 40-yard approach shots to the green. The driver is usually carried for display purposes only ('drive for show') and is most frequently used when a player is out of contention in a match and can thus play with joyful abandon. Using an iron club for your tee shot at a very long hole is good bluffing. It suggests that this course is insultingly short for a player of your power. 'Accuracy, not power, is the key here,' you will declare loftily, but if you shank (*see* Glossary, page 119) on to the railway you're not going to look too clever.

If you do opt for a full or nearly full set in order to make the golf bag look nicely packed, be careful before you splash out on a set of cheap replicas – King Snakes that look like King Cobras, and the like. These go down badly with the club pro and will undo all the good of your investment in Twix and bottled water.

## BALLS

The novice golfer's usual mistake is to carry too many balls. This is self-fulfilling defeatism, and no bluffer should encumber himself with more than six. If you spray the ball around, you will find as many as you lose; and if you lose more than six, you might as well call it a day and walk in. Using an old and extremely beaten-up ball is not a bad bluff, suggesting that several years have elapsed since you last lost a ball. Using balls 'borrowed' from the vending machine on the practice range is not advised, unless you want to be expelled from the club.

There used to be two kinds of balls. The first type was called Balata. This was a 'wound' ball which was much favoured by pro golfers. However, Balatas were rather expensive to make and are now extinct – but there is still bluffing potential to be had in lamenting their passing ('I can't get quite the same degree of spin these days', you might say.) The other type is the 'solid' ball, which is cheaper to make and more than adequate for the golfer who loses balls on a regular basis. Discount stores sell cheap, reconditioned or 'lake' balls, and the pro shop will have a bucket of second-hand balls described, in a fine example of golf-club humour, as 'experienced'. Although they are quite good enough, it will not help your credibility to be seen dipping into the 'experienced' bucket, and besides, having to buy your own lost balls back from the pro is too galling to contemplate.

Beyond the basic distinction between hard and soft, balls are much of a muchness. You do need to know what brand you are using, however, and declare it loudly on the first tee. It is standard form for golfers to introduce their balls in this way. If an opponent extends a hand and says 'how do you do; Maxfli 2', the correct response is not 'hello Max', but 'Top-Flite 4' or whatever your ball is. The idea of the ball introduction ritual is to prevent cheating – that is to say, confusion – by switching one's ball. The famous 007 golf sting in *Goldfinger* (*see The Bluffer's Guide to Bond*) was based on this 'mistake'.

The best policy may be to ask the pro which brand the members favour, and follow their example. When in Rome, etc. Most of the balls you find in the rough will be of that brand, and you can play them as your own without fear of censure or exposure.

## SHABBY CHIC GEAR – LOW-TECH BLUFFING

This approach may lend itself more readily – certainly more cheaply – to the bluffer's cause. Arrive at the club in slightly distressed gardening or shooting mufti, or threadbare cords and a no-longer white cricket sweater, carrying a light canvas bag with a minimum of clubs, sourced via house clearance or a notice board in the village shop. Pretend not to take golf too seriously. After all, you are an old-money golfer who grew up with the game and makes do with trusty old blades. As a breezy opening gambit while loosening up beside the first tee, say: 'These huge modern drivers are so easy to use, it takes all the fun out of the game, don't you agree? Are they are actually legal, do you know?'

The suggestion that your opponent is cheating may knock him off his intended swing plane, or persuade him to leave the driver in the bag. The Rules section of this guide (*see* 'Rules of Engagement', page 75) may give you supplementary ammunition (using the non-conforming grooves ploy, for instance).

Be aware that some genuine golfers use this approach to great effect. They tend to be the club's young tigers or wise owls who have played golf long enough to discover that a small bag is lighter than a big one. They could be bluffing, of course, in which case you may have met your match.

## TROLLEYS

Unless you have adopted the low-tech/old-money/light-bag/short-set bluff, it would be madness to attempt to lift your own bag, and in the absence of a caddie, you will need a trolley. These can be hired relatively cheaply at most golf clubs, but most club members and other regular players prefer their own. And so therefore must you. You might be tempted by a self-propelling electric version, but beware: they come with a handheld remote control that you will never be able to find and a rechargeable battery you will never remember to recharge. The trolley also folds up in such an ingenious way, courtesy of myriad hidden buttons and levers, that you will never be able to open it up again. And since it will be locked to your golf bag, you will either have to carry the whole thing over your shoulder, or hire another trolley when you get to the course. A trolley carried on a trolley does not suggest a high degree of proficiency on the golf course.

## RETRIEVAL AIDS

A telescopic fishing rod for retrieving balls from water hazards may count against the duty-free 14-club allowance (consult the local rules on this). If so, you will have to sacrifice one of your putters. More seriously, it marks you down as a cheapskate, as, fatally, does the habit of searching for your tee after the tee shot.

## TEES

If you disregard all other recommendations in this guide, observe this one if you wish to be respected and taken seriously as a golfer of substance and stature: use only wooden tees. The reason they are made of wood is so that they can be left 'as they lie' to accumulate and reinforce the teeing ground in a sustainable, biodegradable way. Plastic tees are undignified and, if used, should be found and retrieved. This can be time-consuming and irksome, especially if you also have to find and retrieve your ball. Note that playing a tee shot without using a tee peg is a good confident bluff, but can easily misfire, especially when using the driver. When your divot (the piece of turf torn up by your club) travels further than your ball, it is difficult to bluff that you did it on purpose – especially when you're going for distance.

There is probably someone who is worse at golf than you are. If you can find such a person to play with – as an opponent, not a partner – golf will become much easier and more enjoyable.

# TEE TIME

Sooner or later, you may be unable to avoid playing the game. Bluffing becomes more challenging, but is still possible. It is never a bad preliminary bluff to feign injury, limping to the first tee and extending your left hand for the opposite number to shake, with an apologetic mention of your arthritic right wrist, which has never fully recovered from the time you saved your neighbour's dog from drowning. 'It's nothing, honestly. Sure to loosen up in an hour or two. Don't mention it.' Your opponent may be consumed with pity for your misfortune; or his spirits may soar at the prospect of inevitable victory. Either way, his game will suffer.

## THE SWING

The theory behind golf, as any golfer will tell you, is quite simple. Starting with the club head near the ball, slowly bring it back behind your head and swing it down on the same path. Club head hits ball and sends it away straight, true, and singing a happy tune that inspires you to quote the great American golfer Arnold Palmer: 'What other people may find in poetry or art museums, I find in the flight of a good drive.'

A successful outcome merely requires you to make sure that your feet are correctly placed in relation to the ball; your grip neither too strong nor too weak; your arms, wrists, elbows, hips and knees braced, cocked, and bent in the prescribed angular manner so as to resemble an irregular tetrahedron rotating and counter-rotating simultaneously on a fixed axis; your body coiling and uncoiling like a wound spring, smoothly yet powerfully with wrist snap but without snatching or jerking the club as it comes to the ball in an even, accelerating arc, and after the strike, continues over your left shoulder in what is called the follow-through or finish. Remain perfectly balanced throughout, with your eye fixed on the ball, head down and unmoving, and your job is done.

A five-year course in pirouettes and pointe work at the Royal Ballet School under the personal supervision of Darcey Bussell may not be enough to achieve this with any guaranteed consistency, but should get you started on the right track. If we were to select a single hurdle, it would be this: the untrained person is not naturally adept at keeping his head still while all the rest of him is in violent movement.

Most of us can manage, at best, one thing at a time, which is why concert pianists and prima ballerinas are relatively thin on the ground – certainly not numerous enough to populate the world's golf courses and urban driving ranges. The golf shot requires you to do and not do at least eight things in the space of a second, with several (or more) people watching, all earnestly willing you to make a hash of it, apart from your playing partner who is no less earnest in his desire for you to succeed and has told you twice to watch out for the trees on the right. This is equally off-putting.

There are various ways to tackle the difficulty of perfecting the swing. Try them all, ideally one at a time.

## THE NATURAL SWING STRATEGY

Forget everything technical you have been taught about the golf swing. Empty your mind, relax, and play your natural game. Imagine you are splitting a log, swatting a fly, hitting a nail or a computer with a hammer; or performing any other simple task that involves a swing and which you can manage without prior study of an instruction manual. (If you can't think of any, golf may not be for you). You will hit the ball every time, but may have to dig it out of the ground afterwards.

## THE ALTERNATIVE SPORT STRATEGY

If you are having trouble with golf, think of a ball game you are good at, and play that. How about cricket? Take guard (middle and leg, or middle stump, it doesn't matter much) five yards behind the ball and when the starter calls out your name, dance down the wicket like Botham in his pomp and knock the bowler back over his head for a straight six. If tennis is your game, your tee shot will be a deftly executed half-volley lob from the baseline, flat-footing your opponent who is crowding the net 150 yards away. Sport may not be your thing, of course. Do not let this put you off golf. Many successful players are not remotely athletic. Think of Colin Montgomerie. If you are one of those people who can only relax when tidying the house, imagine the ball is an alien clump of dog hair, or a rejected Brussels sprout, to be expelled from the kitchen with extreme prejudice and a stiff broom. 'Sweep it away,' you might hear the venerable BBC golf commentator Peter Alliss say. The advice is sound.

## AUTOBLUFF STRATEGY

It is a truth universally acknowledged that every golfer has two swings: his practice swing, a flowing movement of seamless grace, poise and athletic beauty; and his actual swing, an ugly heave. To put it another way, the golf swing is much easier without the complication of a ball. It is, as the *Rules of Golf* often say, 'a question of fact' that if there is no ball, the club will not be able to smash into the ground six inches behind it, or sail through the air six inches above it. In order to succeed, you merely have to convince yourself that the ball is an illusion. Any good bluffer should be able to manage this.

## ANGER MANAGEMENT

Golf tries one's patience like no other sport. After a few misses, the most phlegmatic golfer loses his cool, slashes wildly with his club, and the ball, which has stubbornly refused to move hitherto, disappears. Whether it sails through the clubhouse window, over a railway line or into a pond is immaterial. There is a lesson here, and it is all about summoning your latent fury, channelling it, and releasing it. You can imagine that you have already missed the ball three times before you address it. Alternatively, think of a typical morning away from the golf course. You have an online banking transfer and a couple of phone calls to make – to cancel your mobile phone contract and change your electricity supplier – before driving round the M25 to check in for a Ryanair flight at Stansted. Angry now?

♛

> The golf swing is much easier
> without the complication of a ball.

Never despair. There is probably someone who is worse at golf than you are. If you can find such a person to play with – as an opponent, not a partner – golf will become much easier and more enjoyable.

## DRIVING

This requires a few lessons from a qualified instructor or brave parent but is quite easy, and as long as you remember not to cross your hands on the wheel, and to stay on the left in two-way traffic, you should reach the golf club in good time for your game. By contrast, hitting a golf ball off the tee with a wooden club (or 'metal') is problematic in the extreme, and playing the fairway wood is an ambitious manoeuvre best left to the expert golfer. The driver is the longest club in the bag, and the longer it stays in the bag, the better. Most golfers carry a 3-wood and a 5-wood, and these are more user-friendly weapons, especially when the ball is nicely teed up in the heavy rough after successful identification. Male golfers should not be caught dead with woods beyond a 5-wood.

## IRON PLAY

Every golfer likes to have half a dozen irons in the fire, and at least as many in the bag. The standard panoply is seven: irons 3 to 9, plus a pitching wedge which counts as an iron and a sand wedge which doesn't. Any more irons than that – a number 2 or a gap wedge – and you are showing off.

The iron shot would be straightforward but for the awkward fact that every club is a different length, requiring a different stance and a different swing. No one can explain this, but the best solution is to choose one iron, somewhere in the middle of the range – between 5 and 7, which suggests 6 as a popular choice – and stick to it. Chopping and changing is asking for trouble. Make sure irons 3 and 4 have some soil on them before you set out, and your opponent will imagine you are in the habit of using them. This marks you out as someone who plays a bit.

## PUTTING

Golfing mortals separate naturally into two groups: group one is reasonably good at getting to the green but can't putt. Group two encounters all sorts of trouble on the way to the green but feels blithely confident about putting, once there.

Group two golfers never understand why group one golfers get so agitated over the simple matter of hitting the ball in the hole from close range. But the point is this: if you have got on to a green in two, three or four shots, the desire to complete in only one or, at most, two more is intense. This induces a state of nervous anxiety, with all sorts of twitches and, almost inevitably, failure.

Group two golfers, rarely on the green in fewer than six shots, are under no such pressure. After their travails in the rough, the woods, ponds, bunkers and other hazards, the green is a safe haven, and on reaching it, they feel positively light-hearted. If called on to putt, they dispatch the ball with one deft and carefree stroke, and in this way often halve and may even win the hole.

So it is the better golfer who gets in a tangle with his putting, adopting and constantly revising strange crouches, contortions and peculiarities of grip, stance and club design. Some grip the putter a foot from its base; others hold it vertical, or screw an extension onto the handle (in the manner of a snooker player) to jam in the folds of their belly in a futile bid to stop it from wobbling during the putting stroke, a job that might otherwise be entrusted to a corset. Right-handed golfers putt left-handed, one-handed, backhanded or with their hands crossed over. All these tactics work brilliantly, until a short putt is missed. Then doubt creeps back in.

The 'yips' or 'twitch', when it sets in, is an awful thing

to behold for all but the twitcher's adversary. Back goes the putter head, smoothly enough; but as it returns to the perpendicular, a sudden jerk twists it to one side. Consumed by the idea that he is going to miss, he does.

It would be cruel to mention the names of Doug Sanders and Bernhard Langer in connection with crucial tiddlers missed before a TV audience of millions, so we won't. It would also be wrong, and an insult to the patron saint of shaky putters, Leo Diegel (1899–1951), an American professional who missed so often from close range that he devised a stiff-wristed, elbows-out style that became known as 'Diegeling'. 'How they gonna fit him in the box?', Walter Hagen asked at Diegel's funeral.

Bluffers tempted to follow Diegel's example should know that Diegeling was no help on the 72nd hole of the Open Championship at St Andrews in 1933. Faced with a putt for victory and two for a play-off place, Diegel left his first putt virtually on the lip of the hole and crouched over the ball in his familiar style – elbows splayed, forearms parallel to the ground – only to miss the final tap-in 'by the widest possible margin' as renowned golf correspondent Bernard Darwin reported.

The example of Leo Diegel is only an extreme illustration of what every golfer knows. In the right hands, no putt is too short to miss. So there would be no excuse in golf for that abomination, the conceded putt or 'gimme', were it not an invaluable tactical weapon.

The accomplished bluffer establishes a psychological advantage by conceding putts of extravagant length in the opening stages of an encounter. The idea is to pressurise the opposition into extending reciprocal generosity, and lower his competitive guard. The sting comes at the death, when the opponent picks up his ball from its spot close to the hole and prepares to shake hands, congratulating himself on a narrow win.

'I'm rather afraid the victory may have to be mine,' you say, 'on account of your not having completed the final hole. I always feel it would be wrong to deprive a man of the satisfaction of holing out for a win, don't you? Such a pity there had to be a loser today, and that it had to be you.'

Golfers do not cheat. They do, however, forget the occasional attempt, or miscount, or accidentally dislodge (never move) their ball.

# HANDICAPS
# (AND GAMESMANSHIP)

In the outside world, a man reveals where he stands by conveying subtle messages such as 'Eton and Christchurch' or 'Tooting Bec Comprehensive and Croydon Tech'. Golf is much simpler: the golfer has a number, or proficiency rating, which tells other golfers all they need to know about his game. Typically for golf, the 'handicap' is a complete misnomer. It is not a handicap, but a great asset, in fact the prerequisite of a competitive game.

Not only does the handicap enable players of widely differing standards to play a close match, which the better player almost always wins (assuming that his opponent isn't claiming a suspiciously advantageous handicap); it also offers the solitary golfer the opportunity to play (and almost inevitably lose) a competitive match against the course.

The principle is simple enough. If your score is 100 on a course where an expert's score ('par') would be 72, you have played 28 over (par). If over several rounds you consistently score about 28 over, your handicap should be about 28; if your score is about 72, your handicap is about zero or 'scratch'. (Technically, you need to apply for a handicap from a club or organisation.) If a scratch player plays a 10 handicapper, he gives him a 'start' of one shot at 10 of the 18 holes, according to the Stroke Index (*see* Glossary, page 121) marked on the card. So far, so egalitarian.

Perceptive bluffers will have spotted that the handicap represents a dilemma. For the purpose of impressing others, away from the course, a low handicap, indicative of an advanced level of performance, is the one to choose. If you want to win at golf, however, a high handicap is more useful; the higher the better, in fact.

The best way to explain this self-confessed lack of ability may be to allude to expertise achieved earlier in life but for some reason – illness, injury, false imprisonment, a stellar career in business, Voluntary Service Overseas – not maintained. Describe yourself as 'a lapsed eight' who would 'be lucky to play to 18 these days, I'm afraid.' This conveys an impressive combination of past mastery, a busy and high-achieving current lifestyle, and charming self-deprecation – and won't commit you to playing well should your bluff be called.

## BANDITRY

Golf is one of those dark corners of the bluffer's world that presents a strong case for perversely pretending to be worse than you are. There are various ways to achieve a usefully high handicap, including deliberately missing short putts during qualifying rounds, and a £20 note stapled to the scorecard before submission to the secretary. But the bluffer needs to understand that no man is less popular on the golf course than the 'bandit', who wins golf matches by means of his unrealistically high handicap. With this in mind, it may be better to concentrate your tactical effort on making the opposition play badly, rather than recording a low score yourself, which will leave you vulnerable to accusations of banditry.

## TACTICS

For the man with club in hand, golf is not the most tactical game. Tactics such as aiming to the left if there are trees on the right, or not hitting the ball in the lake by ingeniously selecting a club that won't get you there, are not tactics as Machiavelli understood the term.

The golfer always gives it his best shot, from the first tee to the last green. He does not encourage his opponent to set the pace in the hope that he might run out of steam. A hole won is a hole won, and on balance it is better to win the first than the 15th, because the match may be over any time after the 10th. If a tap-in for a 'birdie' (one under par) presents itself at the very beginning of a game, a man may be overwhelmed by a sense of doom, but he does not think: I'll save it for later.

Tactics are for the golfer who is waiting for his opponent to play the ball. For him the tactical scope is much greater.

The British writer Stephen Potter went into this in detail in his seminal instruction book, *The Theory and Practice of Gamesmanship*. Suffice to say that Potter is essentially sound on body language, flattery, coughing and clearing the throat (volume and timing), key rattling, coin tossing and jangling, sweet unwrapping, smoking, conversation, apple chewing, insidious suggestions such as 'good luck with that putt' or 'a great driving hole this one, I always think', posture and positioning, nature appreciation (flora, fauna and landscape all have their place), and deployment of the handkerchief. Study your opponent's routines, and interrupt them. Know his weaknesses and exploit them, with strategic allusion to recent fluctuations in the price of gold, pork belly futures or government bonds. Potter draws the line at mentioning tax returns or a man's wife, along the lines of 'lovely surprise to bump into Julia at Fortnum's on Tuesday. You must be delighted that she gets on so well with Henry,' and he is probably right. There are limits. However, you might save the most ruthless tactics for 'dormie three' (a golfing term referring to a lead that matches the number of holes remaining, i.e., three holes up with three to play). In such circumstances, normal rules of civilised behaviour don't apply.

## CHEATING

Golfers do not cheat, and bluffers would not dream of suggesting it – the very thought is unconscionable. Golfers do, however, forget the occasional attempt, or miscount, or accidentally dislodge (never move) their ball, or have the misfortune to trample an awkward shrub lying directly behind their ball, or feel obliged to rescue a tiny insect visible only to themselves and, in so doing, pat down the sand in a bunker. But they do not actually improve their lie, because that would be cheating. A man may be known to be 'a bit sharp', 'bad at maths' and prone to the occasional 'mistake', but he does not cheat, and should not be accused of doing so. Duelling is now against the law. The case of Azinger v Ballesteros may be cited:

**A:** 'I can tell you we're not trying to cheat.'

**B:** 'Oh no. Breaking the rules and cheating are two different things.'

*The Great Gatsby* is another set text. Jordan Baker, it will be remembered, won a golf match under a cloud of suspicion. Her accusers mentioned something about an improved lie. Even in the sewer of turpitude and moral

---

♔

Practice will be alien to you. It smacks of trying too hard, which is bad bluffing, and besides, there simply isn't time for it.

---

bankruptcy that was pre-war Long Island, eyebrows were raised at the suggestion. Then her accusers remembered they had been mistaken.

## PRACTICE

Practice will be alien to you. It smacks of trying too hard, which is bad bluffing, and besides, there simply isn't time for it. Gary Player's famously smug remark, 'the more I practise, the luckier I get,' irritates the hell out of every seasoned golfer, and therefore must irritate you. Golf is his job, so of course he practises. All he is saying is: 'I work.' A better claim might be 'the more I practise, the less easy it is to find excuses.'

It can easily be overdone. 'The amount of practice requisite will vary,' to quote Willie Park (*The Game of Golf*, 1896). 'To begin with a round of 18 holes a day will be found quite sufficient; as time goes on this should be increased to a couple of rounds.' That will do nicely, leaving plenty of time for family life and some putting in the office. Notice that Park makes no mention of the practice ground, practice bunker or practice putting green. By practice, he means play.

Two further points may be made.

## The practice ground

If you practise something you are good at – methodically, with targets and routines and intelligence – you will get better at it. Diligent professionals do this every day. And if you practise something you are bad at, you will get better at doing it badly. In other words, you will hone your bad habits, and get worse. So bluffers should beware the practice ground. It may be depressing, or it may inspire treacherous feelings of confidence which will only be dashed on the first tee or soon afterwards. Either way, it won't help. To all intents and bluffing purposes, the practice ground is a foreign country.

## The practice swing

We have observed that every golfer has a beautiful practice swing, and a ghastly actual swing, the essential difference between the two residing in the inconvenient presence of a ball. So, rather than practising hitting the ball with an ugly heave, practise your beautiful practice shot. If you practise it long and hard enough, you never know, it might just become your swing.

Hear what highly reputed golf instructor Casey Eberting has to say on this subject: 'Speaking of practice swings, don't forget that practice swings around the house and office are a great form of practice, as is mentally rehearsing the movements you're trying to learn.' What else are the house and the office for?

In contrast to an expensive visit to the driving range, practising your practice shot and mentally rehearsing your movements cost nothing, unless you count the cost of new chandeliers, carpets, children and other items damaged by your practice swings.

Golf holidays are mostly an
incoming thing. Foreign golfers
come to Britain to play links golf,
pay their respects and keep the
kilt-makers and shopkeepers of
St Andrews and Turnberry in business.

# THE ART OF COURSE BLUFFING

**W**ily old Scots say all golf courses are pale imitations of the Old Course at St Andrews, and this is true. In the same malty breath, they say there is nowhere like the Old Course. This is also true. You can say what you like about the Old Course, so long as you don't criticise it. You will, naturally, have played it more than once and, at the risk of insulting your companions, you will share with them your inside knowledge that 'as you know, the way to avoid all the trouble is to aim left off the tee'.

Golfers love to go on about how natural the game is. At St Andrews it is. Bunkers grew up where golfers and sheep huddled on a bank scraping away at the grass in an attempt to shelter from the foul weather. Golfing folklore suggests that more bunkers were formed in places where balls driven and sliced by bad golfers finished up, their next shots digging up hefty clods of sandy turf which over time created a sandpit. These are called driving bunkers (they drive bad golfers mad), and at St Andrews they are mostly to be found on the right.

In other parts of the course, slap bang in the middle of the fairway where it would be completely unfair to punish a man for hitting his ball, rabbit warrens collapsed under the tramping of golfers, leaving deep pits from which escape without a ladder is difficult, and the expulsion of a ball with a club almost impossible. These are 'pot' bunkers, because you can't see them, so it's pot luck whether your ball goes in or stays out. Stroll along with your head in the air whistling 'straight down the middle' and you'd be lucky not to fall in and break an ankle.

At St Andrews this was natural, but everywhere else it is a copy. Luckily, few golf course designers have felt compelled to copy the St Andrews speciality pot bunker. They have also abandoned the inconvenient shared green, which leaves the Old Course golfer scratching his head and wondering if it will ever be safe to play his approach shot, and facing absurd 50-yard putts when he gets there. Bluffers should point out that this is not a criticism. It is real golf, as it should be played.

In imitation of the Old Course, golf courses usually have 18 holes, and they divide neatly into categories, which the bluffer needs to understand.

## LINKS

Given a choice, you will always play a links course, because this is where golf grew up – on undulating wasteland among sand dunes. The game is at its most natural here, and played as it should be played, 'along the ground,' (bumpy and unpredictable) not 'in the air' (too easy).

However far from the sea you are, miss no opportunity to express your preference for links golf, which marks you out as a connoisseur and a patriot – there are virtually no true links courses outside Britain.

The most common explanation of the word 'links' is that it is the ground that links the sea and the land, characterised by dunes and an absence of trees – otherwise known as a beach. Bluffers who really want to push their luck might advance an alternative, but false, explanation, namely that the term relates to the advice given by St Andrews caddies to visiting German-speaking golfers on the first tee: 'Links fahren!' (drive on the left).

## HEATHLAND

Golf moved away from the sea when property developers worked out that building golf courses with plush clubhouses was a brilliant way to sell overpriced houses to people in areas previously considered unsuitable for habitation. Walton Heath, Sunningdale, Wentworth and Wimbledon grew up like this, and had the New Forest not been bagged for hunting by William the Conqueror, it would have gone the same way. Between the M3 and M4 motorways, mostly in Berkshire and Surrey, is golf's Golden Triangle, with few bunkers but plenty of heathland and an abundance of gorse, bracken and bankers to avoid. Heathland golf is much to be admired, until you get stuck in the heather. When this happens, say: 'I think you'll find that twig marks the boundary of a regenerative eco-biodiversity zone, so I suppose I'd better take a free drop on the fairway.'

## PARKLAND

Courses that can't be described as links or heathland are usually dismissed as 'parkland.' Serious golfers don't rate them, with their soporifically slow greens and pathetically shallow bunkers, and regard any golf club with the word 'park' in its name as chronically suburban and a poor substitute for the real thing. The main complications on parkland courses are trees. If your opponent gets stuck behind one, remind him of the evergreen golfing adage – 'trees are 90% air, old chap' – duck, and wait for the sound of ball on wood. If you get stuck behind one, play out sideways. Parkland courses also have lakes. Apart from that, they're a stroll in the park.

## DOWNLAND

Golf courses built on hills in the south of England are quite fun to play, with good sea views and long drives possible when there's a brow of a hill 170 yards from the tee and it's downhill from there to the green (or the beach, if you select the wrong brow). Unfortunately, there is usually almost as much upland as downland.

## INLAND LINKS

Also known as links-style, or oxymoronic courses. A good example is Fairhaven, a few miles inland from Royal Lytham, which is actually quite highly rated. But this sort of course generally links a lazy farmer with the idea that it will be easier to make money out of golf than farming. It doesn't usually work. Imagine a parkland course without any trees or ponds, and you will get the picture. Put a brave face on an invitation to play an inland links. It's a game of golf, after all, and the farmer should be applauded for not planting hundreds of acres of oilseed rape or a forest of wind turbines.

## DESERT COURSES AND MOUNTAIN COURSES

These are easy enough to understand, if not play. They are mostly to be found in deserts and mountains, and to be spoken of disparagingly as 'Mickey Mouse golf'.

Use a red ball for mountain golf;
long trousers and a Colt 45 in the desert.

Mountain courses are usually covered in snow; desert courses in cacti, rattlesnakes, wolves and other predatory wildlife attracted by unaccustomed luxuries such as water, grass and edible, slow-moving golfers. Use a red ball for mountain golf; long trousers and a Colt 45 in the desert.

### GOLF COURSES ABROAD

Golf holidays are mostly an incoming thing. Foreign golfers come to Britain to play links golf, pay their respects and keep the kilt-makers and shopkeepers of St Andrews and Turnberry in business.

However, golf can be played all over the world and offers

a useful escape from the family holiday and a welcome distraction from the disadvantages of being away from home. There is also something to be said for playing bad golf courses in good weather in preference to the other way around. Where to do it? This is not a travel guide, but the following might help.

## SPAIN AND PORTUGAL

In order to hold your own when the subject of golf holidays comes up in the bar, you may say that courses in the south of Spain and the Algarve are too crowded to be much fun, but since plenty of golfers are locked in to their timeshare deals, check before you say 'Sotogrotty' or 'Val de Yobbo' too loudly in the clubhouse.

## FRANCE

Perhaps the best foreign golf nation is France. Here, the Duke of Windsor took over from the Duke of Wellington by helping to establish a golf club in Biarritz while taking a break before ascending the throne. He returned after a brief interlude when he found himself with even less to do. France gave golf the great Arnaud Massy who won the Open Championship in 1907, but since then they have not had much to shout about.

The domestic Frenchman does not really have the patience or common sense to be any good at golf, as Jean van de Velde demonstrated when he behaved in a typically dashing and cavalier manner, choosing to take his shoes and socks off and lose the 1999 Open Championship at

Carnoustie, when he could have kept them on and won (Van de Velde hit his ball into the Barry Burn, paddled in to the creek, and considered hitting it out from the water). Not only that, the man was disrespectful enough to laugh about it afterwards, claiming that no one would remember the winner but he, Jean, would always be remembered, as long as water shall run between the banks of the Burn. Wise golfing heads and their double chins shook. Oh dear me, no. Nice man, but he simply does not understand the magnitude of the game, the event and the moment. (Bluffers should know that the eventual winner was the much less colourful, in fact virtually monochromatic Scotsman, Paul Lawrie. Van de Velde was correct; this is often forgotten.)

The cream of French golf plays its game at Chantilly, but there are superb courses all over the place – good value, with some of the best-dressed ladies in world golf and delightful competitions such as an eclectic gastro Stableford Scramble (*see* Glossary, page 121), when a plate of local delicacies and a glass of something crisp and refreshing await as a well-deserved reward for failure at the back of every green. Le Touquet is close enough to Blighty to count as a real links; half close your eyes and Hardelot could pass for the Surrey Heath.

## USA

Golf is a more user-friendly game in the USA than in much of the British Isles, mainly because their 'rough' is less rough, their fairways are more fair, and their greens are more green. Feel-good golf is all very well, but the bluffer should not be seduced by it. Remember, golf has it roots in the British game, and enjoyment is hardly the point. A safe bluff likely to win approval at your club is to dismiss the American game as 'target golf,' a crushing term beloved of links snobs. 'All you have to do is hit the thing over a pond to the required distance and the ball will land on a soft green and stop' – in contrast to the infinitely more creative Celtic experience whereby your ball will be blown or bounce sideways and not stop rolling when it finally reaches the green until it finds a resting place in a bunker or ditch.

American golfers are often further disparaged for a generous and well-intentioned occasional tendency to overlook the botched first tee shot under a system originally known as a Mulligan, but now also referred to as an OJ or a Clinton. Are American golfers alone in this? Almost certainly not, but it will do you no good to defend them at St Andrews or Sandwich.

It may have been an American who described golf as a good walk spoiled, but many is the American golfer who confounds the sentiment by playing the game at the wheel of an electric golf buggy ('cart'), thereby maintaining a consistent level of play from start to finish without breaking a sweat. It might be leisure, but is it sport?

That said, one reason for these hi-tech mobility aids is that Americans have golf courses in places like Arizona and New Mexico where temperatures exceed 100°F. Refuse the cart and you might not make it back to the clubhouse, even if the rattlesnakes don't get you.

The more upscale American golf cart comes with an on-board computer that tells you how far to hit the ball, records your score and invites you to place your food and beverage order for the halfway house. The golf may be absurdly easy, but the technology can be terrifying. Distractions are plentiful on the more expensive courses, with regular interruptions to your putting rhythm in the form of smiling girls driving beverage carts.

Might golf be a more amusing game if some, or perhaps all, of these innovations were introduced at Sunningdale and Royal Wimbledon? You might think so, but don't mention it over here.

And you should know what line to take on the architecture. Many American golfers are usually terribly particular about the brand of golf course they play on, and talk endlessly about the finer points of course design. Are you a Fazio kind of guy? Trent Jones Senior or Junior? British golfers rarely talk about this aspect of golf, preferring to think of their courses as natural. 'God's the architect here,' you will say, when describing the sort of elemental Scottish course which Americans (with honourable exceptions like Jones, Nicklaus and Watson) live in fear of. Course design is seriously low-handicap bluffing and requires a high level of skill, and you will need to bone up on it before a trip to the USA. If you carry it off, the rewards will be high. Meanwhile, if you are unable to avoid this conversation, a good defensive or blocking bluff might be to say courses designed by famous golf champions – Palmer, Ballesteros, Faldo, Alliss, Nicklaus, Norman – are not nearly as good as those made by people you have never heard of (or wouldn't have, were you not such a connoisseur of the minutiae of architectural detailing): Colt, Fowler, Simpson, Dye, MacKenzie, Ross.

## RUNNERS-UP

In Thailand, caddies of indeterminate gender do amazing things with golf balls. Golfers love South Africa: great weather, great wine, great value, shame about the crime statistics. Morocco is a fine place for a golf holiday, but be careful before you express this opinion at your club. Morocco? You may be marked down as a maverick free thinker.

# PASSING MUSTER
# AT THE CLUB

Sooner or later you will end up in a golf clubhouse. Be on your guard, because the members will certainly be on theirs. A siege mentality prevails in these places and inmates consider themselves to be guardians of civilised values extinct outside the precincts of their club. Newcomers are viewed with suspicion and members are constantly on the lookout for opportunities to upbraid or expel them. The comfort and relaxed ambience of a club is a precious and fragile thing, and it is a club secretary's most important duty to refuse membership to anyone who might not fit in. Obviously, basic bluffing skills are required, whether you are hoping to win acceptance as a member or are simply in need of a quiet drink. The following notes give a basic understanding of how the golf club works.

Men of a certain age, who find that the real world has not delivered the succession of pars and birdies they were hoping for, withdraw from it to create an alternative world which runs exactly as the real world would run, in their ideal world. They assume high office, appoint cabinet members, judges, jury and policemen, enjoy power and exercise it tirelessly, pervasively and with ruthless attention to detail. If this was an illustrated book, we would include a photograph of the following sign from a golf club gate. 'Please shut the gate. Fine for non-compliance: £1,000.' Not £10 or £100, but £1,000. Who says? The golf club.

All the things they don't like about the real world – casual dress, mobile phones, fashionable clothing, music, the glottal stop, left-leaning newspapers, the appalling rags young people wear, children, women, jeans, trainers, dogs, bluffers and much, much more – they exclude or ban with notices starting with the words 'Members are kindly requested…'. And if that doesn't work, they pin up another notice stating: 'Members are respectfully reminded…'

The golf club improves on God's work. Nature is a messy and imprecise thing, but at the golf club, all is neat and in its place. One kind of grass for the fairway, a different kind for the rough, yet another kind for the green. Innocent weeds are ruthlessly expunged, wild animals poisoned, electrocuted, whatever it takes. Bunkers are as neatly raked as the rose garden at Kew, and woe betide the man who leaves a footprint in the sand or parks in the wrong space. Members are kindly requested not to wear dirty shoes indoors. Life is not like this, but the golf club is. If you spend your weekends making sure your books are shelved in alphabetical order, you will approve of the golf club.

## JOINING

It is not actually necessary to join a golf club in order to learn golf. You can progress steadily through the ranks –

mini-golf, crazy golf, seaside putting course – until you are ready to take lessons on a driving range where the dress code and socio-educational background entry requirements are quite relaxed. However, it is an inescapable fact that most good golf courses belong to a club and if you want to play golf a reasonable amount – three times a week, say – and keep your costs under control, you probably need to join a club, whether you like its petty rules or not.

There are other reasons for joining a golf club. You might want a social life that you don't have to share with your friends, and you may take seriously your marriage vow: 'for richer for poorer, for better for worse, but not for lunch'. Or you might be in the business of selling insurance policies, or on the lookout for gullible people willing to let you invest their money for them. But the usual reason is to play golf.

People say golf clubs are hard to join, but this is not true. As Groucho Marx observed, the problem is not finding a club that will have you, but persuading yourself that such a club could be worth joining. It is a question of choosing the right one. Applying to The R&A Golf Club in the first flush of your enthusiasm for the game might be a little optimistic. Sunningdale and Rye are said to be quite hard to get into, but there are plenty of less fussy clubs nearby. Be realistic, avoid clubs with 'Royal' in the title, and don't expect too much, too soon. Your first approach may be to join as a country (i.e., absentee) member or a weekday (non-playing) member. That will entitle you to hang around the bar, play a little bridge and billiards, buy a few drinks and refer to 'my club' when out and about doing whatever it is you do in the real world.

You will soon learn to keep your opinions to yourself (entirely contrary to the bluffer's ethos), your shirt tucked in and your phone on silent. Avoid trumping your partner's ace, and in no time you will be invited to upgrade your membership to playing status. Truth be told, most golf clubs are desperate for new members. But they like to get to know you first.

***

> You will soon learn to keep your opinions to yourself, your shirt tucked in and your phone on silent.

If you find yourself with an embarrassment of choice, don't try to set clubs up in a competitive auction, bidding for your custom. Golf is not ready for the 'what I'm looking for at this moment in time, John, is a deal' culture. You must decide. Choose a club that has its first tee and 18th green out of sight of the bar and the pro shop, and you are less likely to be exposed as a hopeless bluffer, with a good chance that inexcusable infringements (taking a deep gouge out of the tee, for example) may go unnoticed.

The annual subscription may seem quite reasonable, but there is also the joining fee to consider. This is often disguised as a debenture or a share or an 'investment', but it makes no difference. You put your money in, and you don't take it out. Basically, it's a Ponzi scheme, with golf. If you don't like it, go somewhere else.

Enter a few competitions and you will get a handicap, and then you're up and running. Ask the pro to fit you in a game. As long as you don't hold up your fellow players, talk too much, make them tramp around the wet grass looking for your ball, try to sell them an insurance policy, or forget to concede any putts inside six feet, they will probably play with you again, same time next week. Welcome to golf, if, indeed, you want to play.

## FITTING IN

Over time, you will learn what makes your club tick. One of the best ways to fit in as a bluffer is to make sure you order the right drink. Sunningdale is famous for its Bloody Mary, but in a sad sign of the times, some members have been known to invite the barman to go easy on the vodka. This drink, if you can call it that, is often known as a Virgin Mary, but at Sunningdale they prefer Bloody Shame, and a bloody good joke it is too. The Honourable Company of Edinburgh Golfers move seamlessly from their Belhaven Ale to their single malt at midday. Royal Wimbledon is the place for a Hill Billy (grapefruit, fizzy lemon, bitters), and Swinley Forest for a Swinley Special (secret recipe). You should be familiar if not intimate with the legendary Pink Jug beloved of the Cambridge Blues at their home course, otherwise known as Royal Worlington. Champagne, Benedictine, brandy and Pimm's No 1 are the main ingredients.

At The Berkshire, where they appear to have named their two courses after vodka – the blue is a bit harder than the red – the authorised refresher is a Gunner. This involves ginger beer, ginger ale, lime and Angostura bitters, a potion which is to golf what Lea & Perrins is to shepherd's pie. Angostura Pimm's is never a bad choice in summer, but if in doubt, summer or winter, rain, shine or course record, make yours a Kummel. This is the golfer's drink. 'Putting mixture. Never up, never in' (a hackneyed golfing maxim which you need to know means: if it isn't struck hard enough to reach the hole, it has no chance of going in).

You must refer to your club, or any you decide to name-drop in company, by its correct appellation. Sandwich is not Sandwich, which sounds a bit cheap, even allowing for home-baked wholemeal; but St George's, or Royal St George's. Never say Harlech: the track you have in mind is Royal St David's. At St Andrews the course that matters is not the Old Course, but the Old. It is a good bluff to say: 'Between the two of us, the New is a better test,' although not a better course: that would be heresy. One or two clubs on which golfing royalty has smiled consider themselves to be more blue-blooded and smarter than the jumped-up House of Windsor and prefer to refrain from using their 'Royal' title. Royal West Norfolk is simply Brancaster, Royal North Devon will never be other than Westward Ho! Don't ask why, but Hunstanton is Hunston. Nobody refers to the West course at Wentworth as the Burma Road any more, so don't.

## GOLF AND WORK

It is a half truth semi-universally acknowledged – its seed planted, watered and lovingly nursed by those in full-time employment who would like to play more golf – that belonging to a golf club is good for networking and business. Unpleasant though it is to pull out the rug, it just isn't done to conduct any business on a golf course. You could dip a toe in the water at the bar after the game, but the water has gin and bitters in it, and by the time all the heroics of the encounter have been told and retold, dissected and comprehensively post-mortemed, your important guests will be far too drunk to remember anything they agree to. So don't bother. The best you can hope for is a card with your bank manager's direct number on it. If this means you don't have to speak to someone at a call centre in Glasgow or Bangalore the next time you have a spot of cash-flow trouble, your generosity on the green will not have been wasted.

## THE INTERVIEW

Prospective fathers-in-law and employers have been known to use a game of golf as a substitute for an interview. If you are invited to take part in such a match, be careful. The best advice is to play your own game, not theirs, let them do the talking and keep your head down (as always). The tricky part is knowing whether to win or lose. It is by no means certain that an older man will want a younger man who has a nasty slice and misses short putts to be his new finance director, or the father of his grandchildren. If he then fails to howl and break his putter over his knee, he may be a bit casual. Golf is a serious business, and there is something not quite right, not quite honest, about those who approach it too light-heartedly. On the other hand… maybe a halved match is the safest outcome.

## THE GOLF SOCIETY

Unfortunately, there are people who are unable to join clubs. It might be their politics, family history, or something in their past, best left undisturbed.

But even these untouchables may decide they want to play golf, as is their inalienable right. They could go to the municipal course, but it takes two to play a golf match, and if they can't join a club they probably also lack friends. So they form a golf society, and give it a plausible name such as the Chancery Lane Golf Society.

At the core of the society is a real golfer who belongs or used to belong to a club, has or had a handicap, and knows how to talk to a secretary and bluff his way around a golf course. He acts as the front man when dealing with the club to arrange the golf society's visit, strides purposefully into the pro shop on arrival, pays all the green fees and blocks the view while the society members, who have changed their shoes in the car park, scuttle to the first tee concealed beneath their umbrellas.

It can't be much fun being a golf society member, knowing that everyone hates you. The reason for this will become clear as soon as you find yourself playing behind a society. Never mind the numerous infringements of the dress code, they are usually terrible players, most of them without the first clue about the rules or etiquette of golf. They are determined to have fun on their day out and take forever.

---

♛

Golf is a serious business,
and there is something not quite right,
not quite honest, about those
who approach it too light-heartedly.

---

These invading golf society types dawdle, shilly-shally, and fail to take the hint when a faster game behind stands menacingly on the tee with hands on hips in the approved manner. Taking their cue from arrogant tournament professionals, they spit on the ground, smoke, chat on their mobile phones, eat bananas between shots and prowl the green for ages before putting, dangling the club between forefinger and thumb as if trying to divine water. After holing the shortest of putts, they indulge in vulgar celebration, with fist clenching, air punching, manual-gear change gestures and coarse ejaculation. Laughter, of all the horrors, echoes among the hallowed dunes – as though golf were about having fun. Instead of vacating the green, they stand around marking their cards and arguing about how many shots they took. Shirt tails out, they swagger back towards the golfers waiting patiently in the game behind, and retrieve their trolleyed bags, which they have left on the entirely wrong side of the green.

If you ring up your pro and request a tee time at 10, he might say 'you can, but there's a society going out at 9.' Now you might question the relevance of this information, but it is highly relevant, because it means when you arrive at the tee for your game, the first two holes will have at least five games of angry members on them, waiting for the last society group to clear the green.

Societies get away with it because clubs need the money, and because real golf societies are often made up of bona fide golfers who like to get together, try different courses and request discounts. They are usually based on professions or trades: pork butchers, taxi drivers, professional hangmen or the like.

Golf Society Man has brought his own laddish vocabulary to the game of golf. Coarse though it is, and frequently offensive, the good bluffer needs to be conversant with it, so as to be able to fit in and contribute to the hilarious repartee. A few of the less extreme examples should be enough to get you started:

**Arthur Scargill** Good strike, bad result.

**Salman Rushdie** A difficult read.

**OJ Simpson** Got away with it.

**Princess Grace** Should have taken a driver.

**Lady Di** Shouldn't have taken a driver.

**Hitler** Two shots in a bunker.

**Glenn Miller** Didn't make it over the water.

**Rock Hudson** Looked straight but wasn't.

**Kate Moss (or name any waif-like supermodel)** A bit thin.

**Dennis Wise** A nasty five-footer.

**Brazilian** Shaved the hole.

**Sally Gunnell** Not pretty, but a good runner.

Moving off with screams of jubilant
celebration before the opponent
has putted is frightfully inconsiderate.
Any Ryder Cup match will show
you exactly how to do this.

# RULES OF ENGAGEMENT

The *Rules of Golf* are laid down, set up, underwritten and overhauled by The R&A in its Scottish lair at St Andrews, the self-proclaimed 'Home of Golf'.

Golfers love to spin out the pleasure of a game for a few hours by discussing some arcane ruling technicality, and the bluffer needs to be able to join in. A close knowledge of the small print can also be an invaluable tactical weapon, as discussed in what follows.

To the uninitiated, the rules may seem impenetrably complex, verbose, long-winded, and weighed down with verbiage, subclauses, appendices and other windbaggery, with much recourse to words like 'deem' and dubious assertions beginning with: 'It is a question of fact whether…'

## APPLICATION

It is a question of fact, however, that the rules are quite logical and consistent, being based on the time-honoured Scottish legal principle of even-handed meanness which, once understood (if not sympathised with), makes it possible to guess pretty accurately what the ruling will be for any situation that may arise in a golf match, from coming to rest in a rabbit hole to being blown off the tee – your ball, not you – by an unexpected squall.

The latter embarrassing accident is less uncommon than you might think, and a ruling must obviously depend on whether the club was grounded before the ball moved. These things are important.

The Rule of Golf (singular) can be summarised as follows. The answer to any question starting with 'Am I allowed to…' is 'No.' If you want to do something that common sense, human rights and fair play suggest is entirely reasonable, you almost certainly can't. And the answer to any objection that begins with 'It seems grossly unfair that…' is 'Welcome to golf, old boy'.

## INTERPRETATION

The rules may not be easy to read, but it is a question of fact that they are easier to learn than golf. Mugging up is a comparatively simple way for the bluffer to establish an advantage over a less-diligent, if superficially more-skilled, opponent. If he drops his ball when he should place it, signs his card on the wrong dotted line or fails to observe the chapter and verse of sprinkler head relief, you may be able to claim a hole or even the match. If this is not possible or appropriate – when playing the club secretary or your future father-in-law, for example (victory would be a disaster) – you can still advance your cause by pointing out an infringement and generously agreeing to overlook it.

Non-conforming (rules-speak for illegal) equipment is

a rich seam. 'Is that a Ping lob wedge you've got in your bag? How clever to have got hold of one before The R&A noticed its converging grooves. Mind? Of course I don't mind, if you feel you need that kind of help…'

Burrowing animals play an important part in many golf disputes, and to be sure of your ground before striding out to the first tee, it is advisable to rehearse the complete list of animals that do and don't burrow, as laid down in the Rule of Golf, bearing in mind that worms ('and the like') don't count. Gophers and salamanders, on the other hand, are deemed to burrow. Applying this knowledge when a ball lands in a hole is a different matter entirely. In order to be absolutely certain that the hole has been made by a salamander (no penalty), and not a worm or the like (penalty), you may need to carry a work of reference or a complete set of encyclopedias.

## STROKE AND DISTANCE

Perhaps the most important rule in golf is this: in any situation, however bad, you can always replay your shot. That's the good news. The bad news is that you must count two extra strokes. The fateful words are these: stroke and distance. Bluffers will hear these words a lot.

### RULINGS

## CASE STUDY A: SLOW PLAY

A pair of dawdlers makes no attempt to let you through, studiously avoiding eye contact and accelerating only as required to keep out of earshot. Eventually you lose your cool completely, play a shot to hurry them along and, as bad luck would have it, one of the blithering idiots gets in the way of your best shot of the day, lies down on the ground and shows not the slightest inclination to move. How to proceed?

**Ruling**

The rules are quite clear about this. You can either replay the shot and try to despatch another old fool, or play the ball as it lies. (No penalty, but don't discount the possibility of a civil action if it lies upon some part of his person). If you are unable to get a clean shot at your ball because it's lying in a pool of blood, proceed as per casual water. Cleaning your ball is permitted and indeed desirable. If tempted to call for help, bear in mind that the use of mobile phones is forbidden at all times. The rules are there to be observed.

## CASE STUDY B: INTERFERENCE

Your ball hits the electric fence protecting the green and rebounds into the hole. Your opponent invites you to replay the shot without penalty. You would prefer not to. The local rules on the scorecard are illegible – you have left your glasses behind. Your opponent offers to read them for you. You don't trust him.

**Ruling**

This is a tough one. Two solutions. A) Buy a spare pair of specs for your golf bag and keep them there at all times (except when you need to read the local rules, obviously).

B) Find someone else to play golf with.

## COURSE ETIQUETTE

If it is important to know, respect and observe the *Rules of Golf*, etiquette is a different matter altogether. Rules are about things you must (or, more often, must not) do; etiquette deals with things you should not do, but there is no penalty for doing them. Indeed, the rewards of doing them can be huge, for the simple reason that they will distract and infuriate your opponent, which is the whole point (*See* 'Tactics', page 47).

For example: 'No one should move, talk, stand close to or directly behind the ball or the hole when the player is addressing the ball or making a stroke.' Try it.

If you do try it, the player is within his rights to ask you not to, and naturally you'll agree, with profuse apologies that will not let up, annoyingly, until your victory is complete.

Having stopped standing directly behind the ball or hole, you are perfectly at liberty to cough, sneeze, light a cigar and send dense clouds of smoke before the player's eyes, or sing an aria (none of these things being forbidden). Many a golfer waiting for his turn to play sighs deeply, without penalty or censure.

Here are some other points of etiquette to read, learn and exploit:

### Speed of play

'Players should play at a good pace.' Self-explanatory. If your opponent is quick, slow down. If he is slow, report him to the club secretary immediately.

## Holing out

'Players should remain on or close to the putting green until other players in the group have holed out.' Moving off with screams of jubilant celebration before the opponent has putted is frightfully inconsiderate. Any Ryder Cup match will show you exactly how to do this.

## Casting shadows

'Players should not cast a shadow over another player's line of putt.' Who would have thought of this ingenious ploy, had the code of etiquette not mentioned it? Accomplished 'shadow-casters' achieve excellent results by holding the flagstick aloft in such a way that the shadow of the flag itself, fluttering in the breeze, flickers over the line of putt, or even over the opponent's face. A voluminous handkerchief may also be used, with well-timed trumpeting. A small mirror ('ball marker') clipped to your belt on a sunny day can also be quite devastating. This really needs to be explained with a diagram and a protractor, but you will soon get the hang of it.

## Conversation

Conversation is a key aspect of etiquette: it is frowned upon, and when brought into play in a timely manner can be quite deadly. Silence is equally effective, when your opponent, faced with an awkward short putt, looks at you with an eyebrow raised in the shape of a question mark.

## Oscillation

Oscillation will be sure to raise its trembling head sooner

or later. The important thing to remember here is that an oscillating ball, in contrast to a ball that moves, is entirely innocent; no penalty can be applied to it. So if your opponent accuses your caddie of moving during his backswing, the riposte might be: 'Are you sure? I could have sworn he oscillated.'

## Flattery

Surprisingly, the rules have nothing to say about the most effective form of gamesmanship, which is so obvious it hardly needs mentioning. Say 'I must say you're driving awfully well today,' or 'That putter of yours is red hot,' and wait for the results. 'I'm terribly sorry, I'm not giving you much of a game,' can be equally off-putting, when you are one down after eight holes.

## Schadenfreude

Bluffers should always conceal their delight when their opponent scuffs, slashes or slices at vital moments in the game. What to say/do? Sometimes nothing at all apart from an understanding sucking of teeth and a shake of the head (both useful ways of stifling a yelp of joy).

Avoid puns (and birthday cards)
based on the ambiguity of golfing
terms such as wood, balls, birdie
and hole-in-one, etc. These mark
you out immediately as a non-golfer.

# HUMOUR, MARRIAGE
# AND ADDICTION

## GOLF JOKES

Astonishingly in a game where self-doubt, neurosis, morbid introspection and obsessive compulsive behaviour are endemic, golfers occasionally find time to relax and sometimes (but not always) share a laugh. In fact, in the cosy cocoon of their country clubs, golfers luxuriate in bottomless self-regard and would certainly not admit to any shortcomings in the sense of humour department. On the contrary, they are forever reminding one another of their favourite golf jokes. New ones are rarely allowed on the premises. Golf is a humiliating enough experience, without the extra indignity of missing a punch line. Bluffers should arm themselves with a few jokes for the sake of conforming, but shouldn't try anything too original.

A good joke told at the right time, for instance just before starting, when your opponent is at his most twitchy, may be worth several strokes on the front nine. One of the best-loved golfing jokes, attributed to Mexican-American player Lee Trevino, who lifted humour to the realm of tactics and arguably won many championships that way, has the golfer holding a club above his head during a thunderstorm and declaring: 'Even God can't hit a 1-iron'.

## DOS AND DON'TS OF GOLF HUMOUR

Avoid puns (and birthday cards) based on the ambiguity of golfing terms such as wood, balls, birdie, hole-in-one, etc. These mark you out immediately as a non-golfer. You might just get away with the frogs leaping out of the lake and on to the green at the sight of an approaching golfer. That's right: next to the flag is the safest place to stand. And so on…

Most other golf jokes focus on the golfer's warped world view, otherwise known as dedication to 'the game'. A matter of life and death? Golf is much more than that.

### Example 1

**Golf Pro** 'Keep a firm grip on the club, fingers overlapping and pointing down. Keep your head still and your eye on the ball. Now hit it smoothly…'

Golfer hits the ball which flies over the fence and into an adjoining road where it hits a motorcyclist on the head. The motorcyclist swerves towards a car and ends up in the ditch. The car swerves to avoid him and heads towards an oncoming bus which veers to the other side of the road and turns over. A lorry coming the other way runs into the back of the car and pushes it through the fence.

**Golfer (distressed)** 'What shall I do?'
**Golf Pro** 'Keep your right elbow closer to your side as you come through.'

## Example 2

A game is about to tee off when a funeral cortège passes on the nearby road. One of the golfers removes his cap and stands silent as it passes.

'I didn't know you were religious,' says the other.
'I'm not, but that was my wife.'

## Example 3 (permissible crudity)

If you should happen to find yourself in more ribald and juvenile company than usual, you may be permitted to resort to the following, but no more:

A male golfer staggers into hospital with a concussion, multiple bruises, two black eyes and a 5-iron wrapped tightly around his throat. The doctor asks: 'What happened to you?' Man answers: 'Well I was playing golf with the wife when we both sliced our golf balls into a field of cows. I found one stuck in a cow's fanny and I yelled to the wife 'This one looks like yours…' and I don't remember much after that.'

## HUMOROUS GOLF WRITING

The supreme chronicler of the gentle absurdity and sweet torture of golf was PG Wodehouse who published his first golf stories in *The Clicking of Cuthbert* in 1916, and welcomed anyone wishing to contact him to 'address all correspondence to: PG Wodehouse, c/o the 6th bunker, The Addington Golf Club, Croydon, Surrey'. Clothes and equipment have changed since 1916, but Wodehouse's characters live on at every golf club in the land.

'I have sometimes wondered if we of the canaille don't get more pleasure out of it than the top-notchers,' he wrote in the preface to his *Golf Omnibus* in 1973, and this is one of the keys to his understanding of golf. In Wodehouse's world, as in ours, the keenest and most dedicated golfers are the worst players.

## THE FILM

Forget about any other golfing film you might have heard of; there's only one bluffers need to be familiar with – not least because it has attained cult status and its better known lines are widely quoted on golf courses around the world. Rumour has it that it is also Tiger Woods's favourite film of all time (after *Cocktail* and *Crash,* you might speculate).

If for some unaccountable reason it has somehow eluded you, it is the 1980 US comedy *Caddyshack* starring Chevy Chase, Rodney Dangerfield, Ted Knight, and Bill Murray. The theme? There are certain eternal truths in the game of golf. The plot? It's really not important, but, in a nutshell, there's an exclusive golf and country club called Bushwood which has to deal with a brash new member and an invasion of fiendishly calculating gophers. So it's not exactly a serious social satire. There's also a parallel plot line about some recalcitrant young caddies, but you can skip over that. What's of primary interest is the depiction of the sort of golf club characters which every golfer will recognise.

## WHO'S WHO (THE PRINCIPAL CHARACTERS)

**Ty Webb (Chevy Chase)** A naturally gifted golfer, the playboy son of one of the club's co-founders, a quixotic dreamer who takes a Zen-like approach to the game and the golf club culture.

**Judge Smails (Ted Knight)** An insufferably pompous buffoon who co-founded the club with Ty's father, and treats it as his personal fiefdom. Not above a bit of sharp practice (on and off the course). Takes a keen personal interest in new membership applications, and despises loud, gauche, nouveau-riche construction magnates.

**Al Czervik (Rodney Dangerfield)** A loud, gauche, nouveau-riche construction magnate with an extravagant line in convertible gold Rolls-Royces, super yachts and golf bags which double as sound systems (among other things).

**Carl Spackler (Bill Murray)** An intellectually challenged assistant greenkeeper with two things on his mind: the destruction of all gophers, and fantasies about bending the lady members to his absolute will.

## LINES YOU WILL NEED TO COMMIT TO MEMORY, AND SOMETIMES QUOTE:

**Al Czervik (on his first appearance in the club pro shop, with his Chinese associate Wang)** 'Give me half a dozen of the Vulcan D-10s and set my friend up with the whole schmeer. You know, clubs, bags, shoes, gloves, shirt, pants. Hey, orange balls! I'll have a box of those and give me a box of those naked-lady tees, gimme two of those, gimme six of those…Oh, this is the worst lookin' hat I ever saw…What you buy a hat like this and I'll bet you get a free bowl of soup, eh? [Sees Judge Smails wearing the hat] Oh, looks good on you, though.'

**Carl Spackler (to an imagined TV audience of millions, swinging at the heads of some flowers with a 7-iron)** 'Cinderella story. Outta nowhere. A former greenkeeper, now about to become the Masters champion. It looks like a miracle…It's in the hole! It's in the hole! It's in the hole!'

**Carl Spackler (spying on lady members putting on the 18th green)** 'Oh Mrs Crane, you wore green so you could hide from me. You're a little monkey woman. You're lean and you're mean and you're not too far between, either, I bet, are ya, huh? How'd you like to wrap your spikes around my head?'

**Ty Webb (explaining his golf philosophy to a caddie)** 'There's a force in the universe that makes things happen. And all you have to do is get in touch with it, stop thinking, let things happen, and be the ball.'

**Ty Webb (continuing the exposition of his philosophy)** 'In one physical model of the universe, the shortest distance between two points is a straight line, in the opposite direction.'

**Carl Spackler (continuing his practised seduction routine to a lady golfer, sotto voce, from a safe distance)** 'Man in a boat overboard. You beast! You savage. Come on, bark like a dog for me. Bark like a dog! I will teach you the meaning of the word respect!'

**Judge Smails (to a recalcitrant young caddie)** 'I've sentenced boys younger than you to the gas chamber. Didn't want to do it. I felt I owed it to them.'

**Al Czervik (on being introduced to Smails's wife at the club ball)** 'Oh, this your wife, huh? A lovely lady. Baby, you're all right. You must've been something before electricity.'

**Al Czervik (aside to his companions)** 'Last time I saw a mouth like that, it had a hook in it.'

**Al Czervik (aside to Smails's wife)** 'You're a lot of woman, you know that? Wanna make 14 dollars the hard way?'

**Al Czervik (to waitress at the club ball)** 'Hey, doll. Could you scare up another round for our table over here? And tell the cook this is low-grade dogfood. I've had better food at the ballgame, you know? I tell you, this steak still has marks where the jockey was hitting it.'

**Al Czervik (waiting for Judge Smails to finish his practice routine in a match)** 'While we're young.'

**Judge Smails (withdrawing his favoured putter for a crucial putt in the match)** 'This one calls for the old Billy Ború. Oh, Billy, Billy, Billy. This is a biggie! Don't let me down, Billy! $40,000 (kissing it). Oh Billy!'

## GOLF AND MARRIAGE

These two important concepts are probably best kept separate. No man has yet devised a satisfactory format for a competitive golf game with a woman (and vice versa); mixed foursomes are dangerous on every level, and golf clubs are not yet ready for civil partnerships, still less same-sex marriages. Even Barack Obama, a most liberal golfer, dared not broach that subject. It would not be a vote winner.

Over time you may find that golf, or at least membership of a golf club (which is not to be confused with playing the game) improves your quality of life to no end. You will spend less time with your family, more with new companions in licensed premises open all hours with billiards, bridge, good if basic food, and poker. This can be a vital aid to the prosecution of a successful and harmonious marriage; and the prolongation of a more typical alliance.

Everyone needs a hobby, but your partner may not agree that golf is as suitable a hobby as wallpapering or the putting up of shelves. Every couple must find their own solution to this difficult situation, which is best summed up by the following reported advertisement from the classified section of the elusive Kensington and Chelsea Conservative Monthly: 'For sale: set of golf clubs, with bag and shoes. Almost new. If man answers, hang up.'

## GOLF AND ADDICTION

Golf is a dangerous game, and even the confirmed bluffer needs to be aware that an intelligent interest in golf can easily spiral out of control and become an enthusiasm, and this phase usually leads to hopeless addiction. Witness the proliferation of embossed leather tee pouches, yardage-calculating gizmos, ball-finding sunglasses and other useless gadgets that appear in the shops before Christmas, along with small books of rebarbative golfing 'humour.'

Bluffers should recognise the signs of addiction. It happens to the strongest of us. How do you know when you are in danger of becoming an addict? You play golf alone, with a head torch for the last round of the day. You buy a new driver every few months and change your putting grip, stance and putter more frequently than that. While others relax in front of the TV, you stand hunched over the hearth rug making a pendulum motion with your shoulders and downstretched arms without – and this is the key symptom – being aware that you are doing it. Wherever you are – in a department store, a cathedral or an office – you find yourself gauging distances and visualising approach shots. Would it be a lofted 9-iron or a crafty bump-and-run to keep the ball under the branches of the ladies' lingerie rail? When booking a hotel room, you make enquiries about the speed of the carpet and request the right-handed room configuration that will give you enough space to chip happily onto the bed for an hour before turning in.

No one has laid bare the phases of addiction with such raw accuracy, or painted a more vivid picture of golf in the home environment than the American writer Richard Armour, in his autobiography, *Golf Is A Four-Letter Word*:

*The Intimate Confessions of a Hooked Slicer.*

In order to save his marriage, Armour resolves to give up the game and joins Golfers Anonymous…'where golfers confessed their addiction and helped one another to go straight (something I had tried for years to do, but there was always that slice).'

When GA does not work, he turns to a psychiatrist. 'Even I could see now, with my head always down, that I was a sick man. "Whom shall I go to?" I asked one morning while shaving. I had assumed an open stance and was seeing how few strokes I could take to get around from one sideburn to another.'

That golf is a metaphor for life is self-evident. Its unfairness, cruel unpredictability and inevitable disappointments issue a unique challenge to the buoyancy of the human spirit. It is when you realise that life is no more than a metaphor for golf that you have a problem. You have ceased to be a bluffer and become a golfer. It could be time to seek help.

# A FEW USEFUL RANTS

Golfers are generally inveterate ranters. Bluffers must be no exception, so you will need to know popular subject matters on which to fulminate at length. Most of them, needless to say, are about how the modern game is going to hell in a handcart.

## THE LOSS OF CREATIVE GOLFING

Golfers have less time, but play more slowly, and seem to have lost all appetite for the more creative approach to golf. After lunch, impress your companions by suggesting a four-ball eightsome. Inviting them to find a space in the diary for a longest drive competition on the roof of the Savoy, or a match from Oxford to Cambridge, without using a driver or satellite navigation, will have the desired effect.

Mention your nostalgia for the golf writer Bernard Darwin's alleged midwinter regime, on a day that included a good breakfast (not before 08.45), lunch and Benedictine afterwards: 36 holes of singles followed by a nine-hole foursome, and bridge after dinner. These days everyone wants to play his own ball, in the dreaded four-ball Stableford stroke play format. What would Darwin have made of that? (Not a lot, one suspects.)

## THE MAJORS

Major championships also merit a prolonged whinge: they offer an endurance test for players and spectators alike, interminable bean-counting exercises with none of the cut and thrust of matchplay. It is a rare event when the last two men walking up the 72nd fairway are competing in any meaningful way. One of them may turn out to be the winner, but the other will have fallen by the wayside and might as well have given up. His token presence on the green is an embarrassment, frankly, to himself and all present. Show your knowledge and fairness by acknowledging the famous Nicklaus v Watson 'duel in the sun' at Turnberry in July 1977. The memory of two days of rare unbroken sunshine on the Ayrshire coast remains undimmed in all who witnessed it.

## THE DECLINE OF REAL GOLF

Yes, old golf – real golf, red in tooth and blade – survives in a few marginal places. Brancaster and a few other traditional clubs insist on a 'two-ball' game. The Halford Hewitt, now there's a golf tournament, and The Amateur Championship too, plus The President's Putter at Rye, where every January a few Oxbridge diehards shiver in a convincing simulation of golf in Scotland. You must lament that there aren't more competitions like them. If you are going to claim to have been there with them, be prepared to answer supplementary questions.

♔

Honest patriotic fervour can be relied upon to spill over into ugly xenophobia and bitter argument after a couple of matches.

## THE RYDER CUP

Bring the conversation round to the Ryder Cup and blood will begin to boil in clubhouses throughout the British Isles and continental Europe. Not to mention across the USA. This competition is the best spectacle, and the best school of tactical golf – a matchplay event which pits Europe against the USA like two teams of bull terriers, the original format (Britain against the USA) having proved unfairly one-sided. Honest patriotic fervour can be relied on to spill over into ugly xenophobia and bitter argument after a couple of matches, with much waving of flags, cheering at lost balls and missed putts, mid-swing coughing, camera-shutter-clicking and all the rest of it, for real. Golf's veneer of gentility peels back to reveal a sometimes very nasty game, and a few not altogether nice people. (This is always a good topic with which to fill an awkward conversational lull at the 19th hole, when you might otherwise be expected to buy a round.)

'You can have the hole and the goddamn cup,' Ken Still

snarled at Bernard Gallacher at the end of a particularly bad-tempered match, but that was the exception. As a rule, the Americans are much better losers than the Europeans, who are still muttering about Kiawah Island (golfers dressed aggressively in what looked suspiciously like Shock and Awe combat uniforms) and the Brookline affair in 1999, when a spectator moved while a European golfer was standing over his putt. 'Outrageous!' fumed the European vice-captain Sam Torrance, and to this day still fumes. The Americans insisted their man in the crowd only oscillated. At the closing press conference, all habitually agree that golf itself has been the winner, and it takes only a couple of years for the special relationship to recover, before the whole thing happens again.

## THE WRONG SORT

Like everything else, golf has been a victim of the democratic process. A certain standard of civilised behaviour was for many years maintained by the long-established British club system: you couldn't play unless you belonged to a club, and you couldn't join a club unless you could play.

These days – your rant might continue – any Tom, Darren or Rory can play golf, and does, on municipal or 'pay-and-play' golf courses that admit anyone with a few clubs and a credit card. (In fact, these facilities serve the bluffer well. The game can be learned, if not mastered, and bluffing skills honed, out of sight of serious club golfers for whom they will be deployed in earnest.)

The rot set in, you will argue, when golf left our shores for America, France and other egalitarian nations. Of course, it is not the new golfer's fault. With no solid grounding in the game, he can hardly be expected to understand the subtleties of etiquette in golf's smarter circles. He turns up at any golf club he chooses, often with disreputable companions, and expects to be allowed to play. Golf clubs can request sight of a handicap certificate, but plausible internet handicaps are not hard to come by and are unlikely to be forensically examined. In the present climate of recession and squeezed pension funds, money talks. Rare is the club whose members would applaud a secretary/general manager for turning away a green-fee-paying, handicap-certificate-holding, bar-and-restaurant-patronising visitor, who is clearly the wrong sort, but on occasions has to be tolerated (*see* 'The Golf Society', page 70).

## THE LADIES' GAME

No chapter about the joys of a good golf rant would be complete without mentioning the other half. Male bluffers must take the view that women should have exactly the same rights of access and priority on the course and in the clubhouse as men. This might raise a few beetling eyebrows, but you can redeem yourself by saying that they should still be banned from the snooker room.

Ladies play a different game, with different rules, on different days. Many of them do it very well indeed, and are happy in their game. Others hatch the idea that they would like to show men how to do it, because that's the sort of women they are. Many men resist, for the same reason. But battle lines are occasionally drawn, and that's when ranters (predominantly of the male sex) come to the fore.

It all came to a head in 2003 when professional golfer Annika Sörenstam decided to enter a championship on the men's PGA tour on the grounds that it was an 'open' event; she was an open-minded Swedish person and bored of winning everything on the women's tour. Some of the men were furious (most notably the Indian player Vijay Singh); others looked on with interest, and expressed polite disappointment when the brave Swede missed the cut. Hawaiian-born Michelle Wie has also assiduously taken on men in successive tournaments, without notable success, but also without any suggestion that she intends to give up.

These are noble attempts to liven the game up a bit, but in truth ladies' golf has never quite recaptured the elan and sheer pizzazz it achieved in the pre-Second World War era, when Gloria Minoprio reigned supreme. This stylish player, of uncertain provenance and no known handicap, successfully entered the 1933 English Ladies Open, and on the opening day stepped out of a dazzling white chauffeured Bentley two minutes before her tee time: 'a tall slender figure wearing a close-fitting, navy-coloured woollen cap, a turtle-necked sweater, and superbly cut trousers of the same colour.' Trousers had never before been seen on a lady competitor. The damned effrontery!

Male club members gnashed their teeth and reached for another stiffener. Nobody had ever seen anything like it.

Minoprio carried a single club in her own image – 'a long-shafted iron with a straight face' – had a caddie to carry a spare club and ball bag, and played in complete silence. It matters not that she found one too many of Westward Ho!'s pot bunkers and lost five and three. By bluffing her way to the highest level of championship golf, Minoprio is the patroness of our cause, the *nec plus ultra* of bluffing in golf and indeed all sport. Bluffers everywhere should applaud her, and have no truck with those male club players who are still ranting about ladies wearing trousers on a golf course.

The annual trip is a core element of modern golf culture that gives long-dispersed groups of friends the perfect excuse to get together for a couple of days and do what golfers like to do: eat, drink and argue.

# MAJORS AND GREATS

## THE MAJORS

There are four major men's annual golf competitions which are bigger and more prestigious than any others – by some distance. They are known as the major championships or, more commonly, the 'majors'. This is because they are 'majorly' important (for those who speak American) and since three of them take place in the USA, they can choose to call them what they like. Any aspiring golf bluffer needs to know what the majors are, when they happen and who the great champions are. Even if watching televised golf has about as much appeal as grinding the enamel off your teeth, if you're proposing to spend some time in the company of golfers and want to give the impression that you have the faintest inkling of what's going on, you need to know the following.

## THE MASTERS TOURNAMENT (BETTER KNOWN AS THE MASTERS)

Established in 1934, this is the first major event on the annual golfing calendar, and it takes place over the four days ending on the second Sunday in April to an accompaniment of exotic birdsong, a background of lush tropical flora, and a constant refrain of morons shouting: 'It's in the hole!' (even when it is clearly some distance from the hole). The Masters is the only major to be held at the same course every year, in this case the Augusta National Golf Club – widely renowned for its liberal and all-embracing membership policy. In 1990 it admitted its first black member, TV mogul Ron Townsend, and in 2012 it admitted its first female members, former US Secretary of State Condoleezza Rice, and investment banker and philanthropist Darla Moore.

**Best known for** Target golf, metronomic approach shots, luxuriant azaleas, the legendary 11th, 12th and 13th holes known as Amen Corner, shamrock green club blazers, and co-founders Bobby Jones (the most famous 'glam-ateur' in golfing history) and the enigmatic Wall Street financier Clifford Roberts (best known for remarking 'as long as I'm alive, all the golfers will be white, and all the caddies will be black'. In 1977, aged 84, he walked out on to the course with a gun and blew his brains out).

**Most Masters victories** Jack Nicklaus, six-time champion between 1963 and 1986.

## THE US OPEN CHAMPIONSHIP
The US Open takes place over four days ending on the third Sunday in June. Established in 1895, and played ever since at various locations around the USA, the first winner was

a 21-year-old Englishman called Horace Rawlins who'd just stepped off the boat. The tournament was then won by Brits for the next 16 years until the Americans figured out how to play the game and dominated the competition, with few exceptions, until Gary Player won in 1965 and Tony Jacklin in 1970. (For relatively new and untutored bluffers, these two were South African and English, respectively.) Recently the tournament has been won in consecutive years by Northern Irish golfers Graeme McDowell and child prodigy Rory McIlroy. However, they spend so much time on the US tour, they're practically American.

**Best known for** Amateur Johnny Goodman winning in 1933 (notwithstanding a three over par 75 in the first round, and four over par in the last); being won consecutively over 35 championships by American golfers (if you include Tommy Armour who was born a Scotsman); being hosted by some of the most beautifully manicured courses in world golf; and having a trophy which has no name (it is simply known as the US Open trophy).

**Most US Open victories** Willie Anderson (a Scot) won four between 1901 and 1905; Bobby Jones (the charismatic US amateur) won four between 1923 and 1930; and US legends Ben Hogan and Jack Nicklaus both won four each between 1948 and 1953 and 1962 and 1980, respectively.

## THE OPEN CHAMPIONSHIP
You will insist that this is better known simply as The

Open, and sometimes, somewhat unnecessarily, as The British Open. It is held over the four days ending on the third Sunday in July. The only major which is held outside the USA, it is also the oldest (established 1860). It is administered by The R&A in St Andrews, Scotland, which has decided that it is the governing body of golf throughout most of the world – except the USA and Mexico, which have decided that it isn't. Always played on a links course at one of nine locations in the UK, it is a great leveller insofar as all-powerful golfers from the former colonies regularly come unstuck in the swirling vortices off the coastline of the British Isles. As a rule of thumb, if the weather is relatively clement (a rare occurrence), it's usually won by an American, Australian or South African; if the weather is filthy, it is usually won by an Irishman or a Scotsman. The last time an Englishman won it was so long ago that nobody remembers what the weather was like.

**Best known for** Consistently terrible weather; a trophy known as the Claret Jug (because it's a claret jug); dark horses who come out of nowhere to win, never to be heard from again (Ben Curtis in 2003); old horses who come tantalisingly close to winning (Tom Watson, aged 59, in 2009); slightly younger horses who actually do defy the odds and win at the advanced age of 42 (Darren Clarke in 2011, Ernie Els in 2012); and also biblical downpours, sleet, hurricane-force gales, sea fog, plagues of locusts… Did we mention that the weather wasn't terribly reliable?

**Most Open victories** Harry Vardon, one of Jersey's most

famous sons, won six times between 1896 and 1914. Famous for saying: 'Don't play too much golf. Two rounds a day are plenty.'

## THE PGA CHAMPIONSHIP

This is the final major competition, traditionally ending on the fourth Sunday after The Open (although it was brought forward by a week in 2007 and 2008 for reasons no one is quite sure of). Established in 1916 by the newly formed Professional Golfers' Association of America, the inaugural competition was mainly sponsored by the Philadelphia department store magnate Rodman Wanamaker. The original prize was a diamond-studded gold medal and $500. The winner in 2012, Rory McIlroy, received $1.445 million and a replica of the Wanamaker Trophy. Uniquely among the majors, the field of 156 golfers must include 20 who are ordinary 'club pros' (although none has managed to win it thus far). And unlike the other majors it doesn't reserve places for amateur golfers (they'd have to win one of the others to qualify).

**Best known for** Being played mainly in sweltering conditions on parkland courses in the eastern half of the USA; not being part of the PGA Tour (which is entirely different); being held at more venues than any other major tournament (but rarely in the western or midwestern states); being known as Glory's Last Shot (as it is the final major); and Tiger Woods being beaten in 2009 by little known South Korean YE Yang, the first Asian-born player to win a major.

**Most PGA Championship victories** Both Walter Hagen and Jack Nicklaus have won five times; Hagen between 1921 and 1927, and Nicklaus between 1963 and 1980.

## MAXIMUM BLUFFING VALUE

Mention the World Championship of Golf, the so-called 'lost' major and you will wrong-foot anybody who professes to understand the history of the game but can't quite put their finger on what this competition is (or was). All you need to know is that it was played in the 1940s and 50s, exclusively in the USA, and that it offered a winner's purse that dwarfed every other event on the professional tour. It was held every August at the Tam O'Shanter Country Club in Niles, Illinois, and was the brainchild of the course owner George S May. By 1954 the prize for the 72-hole championship had grown to $50,000 at a time when most tour events had an average first prize of well below $5,000. In 1953 the competition became the first golf tournament to be shown live on national TV, and had a dramatic finish when the winner holed out with a wedge shot off the green for an eagle (*see* Glossary, page 116). It had suddenly become the most talked about golf event in the world – *Sports Illustrated* sniffily observed that it 'obtrudes like a brass band at a church picnic'. Then, without warning, May pulled the plug in 1958. Apparently he felt that the PGA was demanding player entrance fees which were too high and, in view of the prize money on offer and the national and global exposure he was paying broadcasters for (in those days it was the other way around), he was probably right. The WCG disappeared from the tour, never to return. The expression 'biting the hand that feeds you' comes to mind…

## THE FIFTH MAJOR: THE BLUFFER'S OPEN

Golf is a competitive game for competitive people. Club members have an endless diet of competitions on which to sharpen their golfing teeth – weekly Stablefords, monthly medals, the club championship itself. But many, if not most, club golfers venture from the reassuring environs of their own course at least once a year to play in a competition which is more keenly fought than any other. They are frequently joined by fellow golfers who are disqualified from club membership for whatever reason and not in possession of a valid handicap. In these circumstances, the whole thing needs to stay below the radar of the Golf Club Managers' Association.

The annual trip is a core element of modern golf culture, an agent of social cohesion that gives long-dispersed groups of friends the perfect excuse to get together for a couple of days and do what golfers like to do: eat, drink and argue.

These calendar events are much the same. A few friends have an idea, play it out, and at the end the winner says, 'That was great, let's do it again next year.' The losers say, 'All right then, you organise it.' And to everyone's surprise, he does. In order to prolong the proud moment of victory, no effort is spared. He finds a trophy in the attic, polishes it up and gives it a plinth with his name on. A dark green jacket is sourced from a bankrupt snooker club, or Oxfam, where the profusion of dark green jackets bears witness to the number of golfers who have exactly the same idea. A website is created, and the banal events of 'the fifth major' (as it is always termed) are retold, with wittily captioned photographs, in a feeble style that passes for parodic humour, at least in the mind of its perpetrator. There are thousands of these fifth majors, and every one imagines itself to be unique. In some way, it is.

The weeks before the event are a time of keen anticipation, an email storm of angry bluffing handicap demands, and furtive practice at dusk. Domestic ornaments tremble before rusty torso-twisting, hip-swivelling contortions and everyone's view of the TV is blocked by the golfer's infuriating air-putting routines. Eventually the friends all meet in the selected clubhouse, and start competing to see who can be the last to buy a round of drinks. 'Haven't picked up a club since last year,' is the general refrain. 'Seem to have left my wallet in the car,' says another.

## GOLFING GREATS

Who was the greatest? In order to join in the conversation on a wet day in the clubhouse, you'll need a few key facts at your fingertips.

### League A

**Hagen, Walter** Sharp dresser, sharp talker, successful bluffer; 'you're only here for a short visit, so be sure to smell the flowers along the way.'

**Jones, Bobby** Nice American, and the most successful amateur golfer ever on the international tour (he was a lawyer by profession). Neither the first nor the last to tear up his card halfway round the Old Course. 'Counting only the time I spent in Hell Bunker, I would still have lived for a long time'; also, 'You might as well praise a man for not robbing a bank' (after calling a penalty on himself).

**Morris, various** Mostly called Tom. Mostly related.

**Hogan, Ben** Famous for 'that' swing.

**Vardon, Harry** Probably the best golfer to come from Jersey (apart from, possibly, Ted Ray).

**Palmer, Arnie** Just what the dull sport of golf needed, before it needed Seve Ballesteros.

**Ballesteros, Seve** A legend in your own lifetime but alas no longer his. Golf as theatre. Mention the car park shot at The Open in Birkdale. Don't mention the 'early walking' (starting to walk away from the tee while the opponent is in mid-backswing).

**Woods, Tiger** Those whom the gods wish to punish... classical tragedy, not yet played out (*see* Glossary, page 123). Legendary driver, off the tee and also into a tree.

**Nicklaus, Jack** The Golden Bear (or Bore), badly let down by squeaky voice. Luckily, Nicklaus's record speaks for itself.

**Norman, Greg** The Great White Shirt. Rugged clothing

entrepreneur easily wound up at press conferences by mentioning 'bottling it' at Augusta, and running off with his best friend's wife (Chris Evert).

**Faldo, Nick** 'All my wives misunderstand me' (and they're not the only ones). A more effective communicator when he let his golf clubs do the talking.

**Watson, Tom** Might have won the Open at the age of 59, but it was just too much to hope for. Don't forget the unforgettable 'duel in the sun' with Jack Nicklaus (Turnberry, 1977) in the best weather that Scotland can ever remember.

### League B
**Jacklin, Tony** The best thing to come out of Potters Bar, since the Great North Road.

**Player, Gary** You can't forget Player, much though you might like to. He keeps popping up and giving interviews, to remind everyone how good he is.

**Woosnam, Ian** A little woozy. Welsh. Almost certainly the shortest golfer ever to win the Masters.

**Lyle, Sandy** Once a great ball striker, always a great ball striker. Once a Masters champion, always entitled to have a go. Like many Scots sportsmen, speaks with an English accent.

**De Vicenzo, Roberto** Argentinian gentleman. Signed a card for one shot too many, and is credited with one of the most famous quotes in golf history: 'What a stupid I am!'

**Langer, Bernhard** Never up, never in. Easily done. We've all missed shorter putts than that. (Not with the Ryder Cup at stake, however.)

**Daly, John** Big man, big swing, small problem (*see* 'Golf and Addiction', page 90). Lovely touch for someone so… you know, how should we put it, big.

**Price, Nick** Not the most exciting golfer to watch, but a real gentleman in a game full of fake real gentlemen.

**Montgomerie, Colin** Bad luck Colin. Cheer up old chap.

**Singh, Vijay** Never suggest he cheated.

**Clarke, Darren** Somehow held on at Sandwich. Golf's best-known smoker. Always wears a genial smile. Sponsored by well-known Irish stout, hence many mentions in speeches.

**Sörenstam, Annika** Forced her way on to the men's tour to prove golf has embraced gender equality (and no doubt the next Masters will be held in Lapland).

**Trevino, Lee** Comedy Tex-Mex. Never took a lesson, never needed one (at gamesmanship anyway).

**McIlroy, Rory** Hoping for promotion to the A league. It's only a matter of time.

**T**here's no point in pretending that you know everything about golf – nobody does – but if you've got this far and absorbed at least a modicum of the information and advice contained within these pages, then you will almost certainly know more than 99% of the rest of the human race about what golf is, why it plays such a central role in many people's lives, why it can drive you mad, and how you can pretend to be better at it than you are.

What you now do with this information is up to you, but here's a suggestion: be confident about your new-found knowledge, see how far it takes you, but above all have fun using it. You are now a bona fide expert in the art of bluffing about the world's most frustrating game. Just don't ever expect to master it.

**Think you're ready to shine with your knowledge of golf? Test it first with our quiz at bluffers.com.**

# GLOSSARY

**Address**
1. Links View, Westward Ho! isn't bad.
2. The beginning of the shot. Wiggling the head to and fro is fine; you can shift your feet, twitch your bottom, clench and unclench your right hand, and waggle the club all you like. But once you have touched the ground with the club head, you are deemed to have addressed the ball. Whatever you do next will count as a shot, so you may as well hit the thing.

**Air shot** A miss. Also practice shot (*see* 'Handicaps (and Gamesmanship)', page 50).

**Albatross** Large bird, rarely seen. Also a score of three under par on an individual hole. It's never going to happen so don't worry about it.

**As it lies** Where the ball comes to rest: usually in a small hole, burrow or divot, or behind a tree, wall or other obstruction. In their fairness, the *Rules of Golf* usually require a ball to be played as it lies, but winter rules may help, by allowing the ball to be 'cleaned' (moved).

**As we lie** This has nothing to do with lying, but is something golfers say to one another as a reminder that at this stage of the hole, their contest could not be more finely balanced. Typically the player whose ball sits a couple of inches from the hole after two shots smilingly says to his opponent, when the latter's second lands in a bunker: 'As we lie, I think?'

**Back spin** Spin is the professional's secret, which does not make the game more difficult for him than for us, as is widely supposed, but easier. The spinner can land the ball anywhere on the green, and it will stay there. The amateur has a thin target landing strip of about three yards at the front of the green – any shorter and he is in the sand, or water; any longer, and he bounces and rolls over the back. Ask any pro to teach you how to spin the ball, and he will laugh, patting you on the shoulder patronisingly.

**Bad lie** You soon get used to this in golf. Typical examples are: 'I drove the ball 260 yards,' 'What a shame one of us had to lose,' and 'I don't care how badly I play, it's just great to be here.'

**Baffy** Ancient name for a 4-wood. The most experienced caddie can be put in his place by a request for a baffy.

**Balls** Correct response to an opponent who suggests that you placed your marker in front of the ball, and replaced the ball in front of the marker.

**Birdie** One shot under par. Rare, but worth mentioning. Golfers go on about it for ages.

**Bisque** An extra stroke, generously donated over and above the handicap allowance, and used as a desperate measure by golfers who are in the soup – dormie three down, for example, and bunkered. 'At this point, we have to use our bisque.'

**Brassie** Archaic name for a 2-wood with a brass sole. Careful how you say that to the club captain.

**Bunker** A deep hole full of sand, broken bricks and poisonous snakes, with an overhanging cliff face on the side nearest the green. Americans call bunkers traps, and this is the trap: the club head must not touch the ground before the shot. If you can't address the ball, how on earth are you supposed to hit it?

**Caddie** Now rare. Using a caddie marks you out as a confident golfer who plays well enough not to be put off by bad advice and a scornful attitude.

**Cleek**
1. An old iron club corresponding to the modern 1- or 2-iron.
2. The committee (as in 'clique', much beloved in golf culture).

**Divot** A lump of fairway that is a bad thing if it travels farther than the ball, but a good thing if your opponent's ball comes to rest in one.

**Dog-leg** A hole which bends sharply to the right or left and offers players the choice of cutting the corner or playing safe. So long as you don't declare your intention in advance, any kind of shot can be presented as deliberate.

**Draw**
1. A shot that moves out to the right and then in again (reverse the instructions if you're left-handed). All golfers aspire to this 'shape', but its superiority to the straight hit has yet to be conclusively demonstrated, unless there is a tree in the way.
2. A hook.

**Driver** A straight-faced wooden club which is no laughing matter. The idea is to hit the ball a long way, but this may not be an advantage if it goes in the wrong direction. As a rule of thumb, when tempted to use the driver, don't.

**Eagle** Two shots under par. It's not going to happen.

**Fade**
1. The opposite of a draw, and much less fashionable.
2. A slice.

**Fairway** The narrowest part of the golf course, and the most exposed. It is hard to conceal your actions from public view or find anything to blame for a bad shot. Luckily the grass is kept very short and the ball usually rolls off the fairway into the rough, where excuses abound.

**Fluff** Easily removed from the green, but make sure you don't press the grass (two stroke penalty).

**Foozle** A duff, fluff, mishit, pear-shaped, complete Horlicks. Popular with polite Americans, it belongs to another age and should be allowed to rest in peace.

**Fore** 'Watch out!' Also: 'Get a move on you old fool!'

**Foursome** A team game of golf with two balls in play (obviously).

**Free drop** Rarely offered to an opponent before he has conceded the hole. The subtext is: 'I may call in the favour later.'

**Gimme** A short putt you think you may well miss and invite your opponent to concede. If he is more than four up, he might.

**Good (also okay, right, all right, have, give)** Word, if uttered on green, likely to be seized on by your opponent as evidence that a putt has been conceded.

**Green** An area of smooth grass with a hole in the bumpy bit.

**Green fee** The cost of a round of golf. Incalculable, financially and emotionally.

**Greensome** A golf match that can't decide if it's going to use two or four balls.

**Ground under repair** Newly dug graves, archaeological zones and other parts of the course where golfers have had a spot of bother.

**Hazard** The last place you want to be on a golf course; more or less anywhere in an arc of 180 degrees of a golfer preparing to hit a ball. Or even 360 degrees if it hits his foot.

**Hole out** Hit the ball into the hole. This is the general idea of golf, but many players go complete rounds without achieving it.

**Honesty box** For green fees; always empty.

**Hook** An indecisive shot that starts off on the right and ends up miles to the left, usually lost, and sometimes known as a Stansgate (aka Tony Benn, the former viscount of the same name). When played by a left-hander, the hook travels from left to the extreme right and may be called a Blair.

**Iron** Metal rarely used in golf, although when clubs were made entirely of wood, those that were not woods (or putters) had iron heads.

**Jigger**
1. An inn in St Andrews; a bit touristy and overpriced these days.
2. (obsolete) Narrow-bladed club used for short shots to the green.

**Lay up** Tactical golf shot to save going through the back of the green. If your approach shot from 100 yards out lands well short, you laid up.

**Lie**

1. Describing your game when you get home (to a keenly uninterested spouse).
2. Ground condition where the ball lies, usually bad. Improving the lie is bad form, but one way to get away with it is to pick the ball up 'to check that it's mine'.

**Lost ball** A ball should be declared lost if not found in five minutes. After four minutes and 50 seconds of searching, wave the game behind through and you may be able to look for another five minutes. If you still can't find it, try looking in your trouser leg or pocket. It might just have got caught in there.

**Mashie** All-purpose iron club – 5-iron, roughly – with many variations. Mashie niblick, spade mashie, fork mashie, mashie spoon, mish mashie, steam iron, any old iron.

**Medal** A monthly golf competition won by other, annoyingly consistent people (who rarely play anywhere other than their local course). Every hole must be completed, and every shot counts. This may be fair, but it's no fun.

**Niblick** Yet another old iron club with a sloping face, quite like a 9-iron but much more evocative. Golf writer Bernard Darwin made a career out of the phrase 'an angry man and his niblick'.

**Par** The score you ought to make if you were any good.

**Play through** When looking for a ball, resting or playing with someone who needs 14 practice strokes for every shot, etiquette requires you to invite the game behind to overtake. Those playing through will say 'thanks very much' before making a complete hash of their shots, with lost balls in much the same location as yours. It is then hard to know how to proceed, but there may be yet another game coming up behind that can be waved through, ultimately leading to total paralysis on the course.

**Provisional** It does no harm to say 'provisional' before every shot, to indicate that you are probably going to lose the ball but, just in case, here goes.

**Putt** The only part of the game that matters. Golf has been described as a game of 'ifs and putts'. About its vital importance in the game you will say: 'Drive for show, putt for dough.'

**Rake** A useful tool for stopping your ball before it rolls in to the bunker. Send the caddie forward to arrange the rakes before you drive.

**Ray, Ted** British golfer (1877-1943). When asked for advice on how to hit the ball farther, he replied: 'Hit it harder.'

**Rescue club** A broad-headed club – probably a wood, but it's hard to tell these days – designed to get a ball out of a bad lie. The most effective design has four fingers and a thumb.

**R&A, The** Mystifying appellation for an organisation which oversees the *Rules of Golf* (among other things). Also a popular description for an exclusive golf club in St Andrews,

Scotland, which doesn't actually own a golf course, and is apparently an entirely separate entity. Confused? Wait until you try reading the *Rules of Golf.*

**Scramble, or Texas Scramble, or Texas** A tedious team game devised by good golfers and patronisingly described by them as 'great fun'. The rules allow bad players to take part but not count or influence the outcome.

**Scratch** A golfer whose handicap is zero (i.e., someone who does not need to bluff).

**Shank** A dreadful mishap. No one knows what causes it, but the symptoms are familiar to all. When it happens, you may be able to recoup some credibility by mentioning the 'hosel', the part of the club usually blamed for sending the ball sideways. You may need the pro to 'realign' it.

**Slice** *See* 'Fade.'

**Spoon** Now called a 3-wood. Golfers are fond of exchanging spoonerisms such as 'you chucking feat'.

**Stableford** A friendly stroke play scoring system popular among bad golfers. You can make a complete hash of a hole, or take a few holes off, and still win.

**Stance** Unnatural body position recommended by many teaching pros.

**Stroke index** Nothing to do with loss of brain function in this context (although it could be). An extremely complicated mechanism for working out when to give your opponent, who has a higher handicap than you, an extra stroke (or two).

**Stymie** Blocking manoeuvre. The stymie is a rare example of a golfing term that has completed the journey into everyday life, and left golf behind. The tactic of using your ball to block your opponent's route to the hole, as in a snooker, was removed from golf in 1952, and as a result few golfers now bother to master the art of the swerved putt.

**Tee**
1. Untidy area littered with bits of coloured plastic, sweet wrappers and vulgar advertising notices at the beginning of each hole.
2. Small plastic or broken wooden peg used to make holes in trouser pockets, fill ashtrays in bedrooms, break washing machines and record the score when you've lost all your pencils. The ball may be placed on a tee at the beginning of each hole. That's all the help you are going to get, so you might as well use it.

**Twitch** Putter's disease best cured by regular infusions of alcohol.

**Twosome** A small, intimate dinner party, not to be confused with competitive golf between two players, usually described as a 'game of golf' or 'match'.

**Wedge** A club with a steeply sloping face invented by the champion show-off Gene Sarazen and designed for flashy trick shots that send the ball high in the air without forward progress.

**Whiff** An air shot in America. Many golfers take umbrage at the suggestion of a whiff, and it is easy to see why.

**Winter rules** The golf club is a relaxed place during the winter months. Members are allowed to wipe the mud off their ball before hitting it. And then replace it in a more advantageous lie.

**Woods**
1. Long-haul clubs made of graphite, Kevlar, carbon fibre, steel or almost anything except wood.
2. Tigerish golfer who scored too much, too often and in all the wrong places, and had to take a break and seek therapy after he drove his car into a tree.

**Your honour** A common golf term for 'after you'. 'Your honour, your honour' was said repeatedly to Judge Smails in the cult golf film *Caddyshack* (*see* page 86). The joke didn't wear thin.

# BLUFFING NOTES

## Bluffing Notes